HOW TO SPEAK YOUR SPOUSE'S LANGUAGE

Does a wall of misunderstanding stand between you and your spouse?

Clear communication is an essential element of a happy marriage. When you fail to speak the same language as your husband or wife, your relationship is sure to suffer. H. Norman Wright shows you how to keep the lines of communication open by learning the language of the one you love. Reflecting his counseling expertise, the author provides numerous case studies that verify the effectiveness of his counsel. Here is a fascinating discussion of all aspects of talking and listening: vocal components, facial expression, body language, prayer, and more. Norman Wright enables you to see how each plays a role in determining your perceptions and clarifying your understanding of each other. Would you like to enjoy the satisfaction of communicating in a positive, loving manner? Enrich your relationship by discovering *How to Speak Your Spouse's Language*.

By H. Norman Wright:

The Christian Use of Emotional Power
The Living Marriage
Making Peace With Your Past
How to Speak Your Spouse's Language

HOW TO SPEAK YOUR SPOUSE'S LANGUAGE

H. NORMAN WRIGHT

Chosen Books

A Division of Baker Book House Co
Grand Rapids, Michigan 49516

Unless otherwise identified Scripture quotations are from the New American Standard Bible, © The Lockman Foundation 1960, 1962, 1963, 1968, 1971, 1972, 1973, 1975, 1977.

Scripture quotations identified KJV are from the King James Version of the Bible.

Scripture verses marked TBL are taken from *The Living Bible*, Copyright © 1971 by Tyndale House Publishers, Wheaton, Ill. Used by permission.

New Testament Scripture quotations identified AMP are from the Amplified New Testament © The Lockman Foundation 1954-1958, and are used by permission.

Old Testament Scripture quotations identified AMP are from AMPLIFIED BIBLE, OLD TESTAMENT, Copyright 1962, 1964 by Zondervan Publishing House, and are used by permission.

Scripture quotation identified MLB is from THE MODERN LANGUAGE BIBLE—THE NEW BERKELEY VERSION IN MODERN ENGLISH, Copyright 1945, 1959 © 1969 by Zondervan Publishing House, and are used by permission.

A NEW BEGINNING, by Gary Emery, Ph.D. Copyright © 1980 by Gary Emery, Ph.D. Reprinted by permission of SIMON & SCHUSTER, Inc.

RAISING A RESPONSIBLE CHILD, by Don C. Dinkmeyer and Gary D. McKay. Copyright © 1973 by Don C. Dinkmeyer and Gary D. McKay. Reprinted by permission of SIMON & SCHUSTER, Inc.

Excerpt from THE SECRETS MEN KEEP by Kenneth Druck, MD and James Simmons. Copyright © 1985 by Ken Druck, MD and James Simmons. Reprinted by permission of Doubleday & Co., Inc.

This volume was originally published under the title *Energize Your Life Through Total Communication*

Library of Congress Cataloging-in-Publication Data

Wright, H. Norman.
How to Speak Your Spouse's Language

1. Communication (Theology)   I. Title.
BV4319.W74   1986   248.4   86-20359
ISBN 0-8007-5280-5

Copyright © 1986 by H. Norman Wright
Published by Fleming H. Revell
a division of Baker Book House Company
P.O. Box 6287, Grand Rapids, Michigan 49516-6287
All rights reserved

Fifth printing, July 1993

Printed in the United States of America

Contents

HOW TO SPEAK YOUR SPOUSE'S LANGUAGE

One

Speak My Language _____

Do You Speak the Same Language?

It was hard not to notice the young couple sitting at a restaurant table, looking at each other with rapt attention. The noise and talking at other tables did not distract them. They talked together as though they were the only couple there. As he spoke, her facial expression and the intensity of her gaze indicated that she devoured every word. When she responded, he nodded in agreement, raised his eyebrows on occasion, and looked intently into her face as she shared with him. The intensity of their personal attention to each other indicated a couple very much in love.

A man at a nearby table observed them. As they finished

their dinner conversation and got up to leave, he stopped them.

"Pardon me," he said. "Could I ask you a question?"

They stopped and smiled. "Of course, what is it?"

"I couldn't help notice the two of you talking together," the man replied. "You both seemed to be hanging on every word. Do you feel you can communicate so that you really know what the other person means? Are you really able to grasp what your partner feels and believes? Do you—"

The couple interrupted him with laughter. "Of course, we do," the woman said. "There is absolutely no problem in the way we communicate. We're on the same wavelength. That's one of the reasons we're so attracted to each other. Communication is *no* problem for us!"

Two weeks later the couple walked down the aisle of their church and committed themselves to each other for life, and they communicated happily ever after. *Or did they?*

Five years later. Same restaurant. Same couple. Same man seated at a corner table, watching the couple talk. This time they speak, but do not communicate. He notices them interrupting each other, shaking their heads, or rolling their eyes upward in disgust. At times they look angry. The husband glances around the room as the wife continues to talk to him. She raises her hands in a frustrated manner, and her voice begins to carry to adjacent tables. He shakes his head, and his eyes convey unbelief and confusion. Soon they leave their table and begin walking out of the restaurant. The man observing them intercepts them and says, "May I ask you a question?"

The couple stop, hesitate, look at each other and then back at the man, with puzzled expressions.

The husband responds, "Well, . . . all right. What's your question?"

"It's very simple," the man replies. Then he repeats the questions asked five years earlier. "I couldn't help but notice you talking. Do you feel that you can communicate so that you really know what the other person means? Are you really able to grasp what your partner feels and believes? Do you—?"

Both husband and wife interrupt the man, and she exclaims, "Communicate! I try, but he doesn't listen. Either his mind is fried, or he doesn't have the capacity to understand simple language. You'd think I was talking to a stranger. And—"

Her husband breaks in. "Half the time I don't even understand what she's trying to say. You'd think she's speaking a different language. We can't communicate! We talk right past each other. She sees things so differently from the way I do. And she talks incessantly. On and on and on! I don't know what she's trying to say." They begin arguing, and the man quietly slips into the background as the couple walks away, each voice oblivious to the fact the partner isn't listening. Years ago they thought they could communicate, but now. . . .

Let's listen in on two people discussing a business deal.

George: "I don't understand it. I worked and worked on the proposal for weeks. I did my homework, covered every angle, and made what I thought was a great presentation."

Fred: "Well, what happened then? Why did they go for the competitor's proposal?"

George: "I can't figure it out. It's got me stumped. Especially since I have a copy of the other company's bid. It's no different from ours. In fact, we came in a bit lower in cost. I don't understand it."

Fred: "There's got to be a reason. How did your presentation go?"

George: "I felt it went well. It didn't take long. They didn't ask many questions. I made it very clear, and they seemed polite and interested. . . . I thought I had it sewed up. I was so sure I had it, I waited around until after our competitor's presentation. I thought they would want to sign then."

Fred: "Why? What made you think they were ready?"

George: "The other presentation was three times as long. It was complicated and confusing. I don't know why they spent so much time in there. I was sure we were on the same wavelength, and they would go with us. . . ."

But George was *not* on the same wavelength when he made the presentation. Oh, what he presented was good, but he failed to connect with his listeners. Why? *Because he wasn't speaking their language!* They were much more comfortable with the other person's presentation, and a rapport was established. That's why they signed!

A husband and wife sit in their softly lit family room, listening to the sounds of an orchestra, coming from the stereo. The room is comfortable and a few pleasant smells from dinner linger in the air. They sit across from each other, looking at the plans for remodeling one section of their home.

Husband: "If you will look over the new design and room arrangement, you will see very clearly that I've focused on the suggestions that you mentioned the last time we looked these over. I just can't see what is bothering you about these changes now."

Wife: "I don't know. I just keep getting the feeling that something in this room is missing. I can't define it. We need to get a better handle on something."

Husband: "I think you're just stuck in your own point of view. You remember something from your home when you were a kid, and you'd like to see it here. Look at it from a different perspective. Then you'll see how this arrangement will be so much better than what you're talking about."

Wife: "No. I don't think you have the proper feel for what this room can express. You need to get in touch with this arrangement from my point of view. Don't you understand what I'm telling you?"

What do you think? Will they understand each other? Or are they speaking two different languages?

Two college students are talking over dinner. One says, "You know, I really feel comfortable talking with the new college minister. What a difference between him and the old one. This guy understands me. I can just tell it. We really seem to speak the same language."

His friend replies, "Yeah, I know what you're saying. He shows an interest and lets you know that he's really tuning into you. He does seem to speak our language."

There it is!

There *what* is? One of the greatest secrets of effective communication and conversation. Follow this principle, and you will be amazed at the results: *Speak the same language as the other person!*

What does that mean? Am I saying you should find people who talk the way you do and in the same manner? That these are the ones you can really communicate with? *No*, I don't mean that at all. That would limit you to a few people. Instead I'd like to show you how to be flexible and learn the language of those with whom you come in contact. That allows you to effectively communicate with almost everyone.

Communication and a Foreign Language

Have you ever traveled in a foreign country? There are two types of travelers: the colonizer and the immigrant. The colonizer wants to visit another country, but sees it from his own perspective instead of experiencing it from the inhabitants' point of view. As he enters the country he looks for signs in his own language and seeks out people who speak his own tongue. He endeavors to find the familiar and fails to venture into uncharted territory. He doesn't branch out and learn any words in this foreign language. In fact, this traveler becomes irritated when he can't read signs for the bathroom or understand the menu. Instead of asking for help or learning a few helpful phrases, he becomes upset. He is dependent on others from his own country, who can interpret for him and guide him around. When he talks to local residents, he approaches them in his own language, and they either respond with puzzlement or say a few words they have learned and point him in some direction. Our traveler ends up creating an unpleasant experience for himself and can't wait to get back to familiar territory. He returns home with the attitude that the people of that country are not very friendly. They weren't interested or helpful. If they had been, they would have provided messages in his language and learned his language in order to help tourism.

Quite often colonizing nations do this. They transport their own language, customs, and monetary system to another country and force the people there to become like them.

The immigrant traveler is quite different. He is somewhat of an adventurer. In advance he prepares for his trip by orienting himself to this foreign culture. He reads books about the culture, customs, and history of the country and attempts to learn everyday phrases of this new language. In order to be able to converse with the native population, he may even take a class in their language before he leaves. When he arrives at his destination, he is eager to discover all he can. He looks for historical sites, tries all the new foods, reads as much as he can in the language of the country, and uses his newly formed verbal skills where possible. He may even enjoy living with a family of that country for a while in order to fully capture the flavor of this new world.

As the immigrant attempts to speak this new language, the people respond in a helpful manner. They help him pronounce strange words. Often, if they are adept in the traveler's language, they will begin to speak it in order to make him more comfortable. They seem delighted that this person has made an attempt to learn their language, and they can both laugh at some of his mispronunciations. When the immigrant returns home, he is bursting with enthusiasm and stories of his experiences. He says the people there were so friendly and open and interesting. They were delightful!

But wait a minute! Both the colonizer and the immigrant went to the same country and encountered the same people. Why the difference in response? Very simple. The immigrant was willing to learn about the culture of the people and learn to speak their language. As he attempted to speak the way they did, the people responded positively to his attempts and tried to make it easier for him by speaking his language in return.

If you really want to communicate, initially don't put the responsibility on the other person to understand you. Reach out and attempt to understand the other person first, and that will free him up to respond to you!

How can you do this? In this book I will provide you with the principles for effective communication. They are simple, and they work! If the way you are communicating isn't working, what have you got to lose by trying a new method? If you feel your communication *is* working, let's make it even more effective.

By the way, what are you? A colonizer or an immigrant?

Speak my language and I will respond to you.

Energy Builders

1. Have you ever had a situation in which you had great trouble communicating with someone else? What happened? Were you both speaking the same language?

2. Have you ever traveled to a foreign country? Did you have trouble communicating? Why or why not? Were you a colonizer or an immigrant?

3. What will you do this week with the information in this chapter? Describe how your communication will be different.

Two

The Power
of Listening _____

The best communicators do not rely upon their mouths; instead they rely upon their eyes and their ears! That's right—the outstanding communicators are those who listen. Sure, that makes sense, but what about *eyes?* Yes, I meant *eyes*, because you listen as much with your eyes as you do with your ears (or you should!). In fact, right now you are listening with your eyes and perhaps saying the words to yourself. In our verbal conversations we also listen with our eyes as well as our ears. But we'll discuss that later. First let's look at some facts.

Fact: There are few good listeners in the world today! Most of us suffer from a state of deafness.

Fact: Listening is a skill that can be learned!

Fact: Many conversations today are nothing more than dialogues of the deaf.

Fact: There are correctable reasons why people struggle with listening.

Fact: Listening is a biblical principle for living life to the fullest.

Fact: In a conversation, the person listening has more control or power than the person speaking.

Be One of the Few Good Listeners. As we learn to listen, we learn to understand and live life. We build our relationships on caring enough to listen to another person, and listening brings about changes in both the person listened to as well as the one listening. When you listen to someone, you send that person the message that you believe he or she has something worthwhile to say, that he or she has value. It is an act of love and caring. Listening helps us to adventure into the life of another person. If you are a good listener, more people will invite you to be a guest in their lives.

You Can Learn to Listen. Yes, listening is a skill to be learned. Your mind and ears can be taught to hear more clearly, your eyes can be taught to see more clearly. Jesus said:

> Therefore I speak to them in parables; because while seeing they do not see, and while hearing they do not hear, nor do they understand. And in their case the prophecy of Isaiah is being fulfilled, which says, "You will keep on hearing, but will not understand; And you will keep on seeing but will not perceive; For the heart of this people has become dull, And with their ears they scarcely hear, And they have closed their eyes Lest they should see with their eyes, And hear with their ears, And understand with their heart and turn again, And I should heal them."
>
> Matthew 13:13–15

Our pattern for *how* we are to listen is very simple and clear from Scripture. "He who gives an answer before he hears, It is folly and shame to him" (Proverbs 18:13). ". . . Let every man be quick to hear (a ready listener) . . ." (James 1:19 AMP).

Listeners Have More Influence. Are you aware a listener controls the conversation, not the speaker? Probably not, since most of us operate under the myth that the more we talk, the more we influence the listener. If both people in a conversation believe this, the talking escalates and becomes more intense, which is quite sad, because the words fly through the air with nowhere to land. Deafness prevails!

What do I mean by the statement that the listener controls the conversation? Compare the listener to the driver of a car. The one talking is like the engine. The engine provides the power, but the person at the wheel has the power to decide where the car will go. You, the listener, can give direction and guide the flow of the conversation by the statements you make and by the questions you ask.

Questions such as the following can guide and lead:

"That's an interesting thought. Can you tell me a bit more how that will . . . ?"
"Does that mean . . . ?"
"If I understand what you are saying. . . ."

This last statement is what is called paraphrasing. It reinforces the person talking so that he or she will continue to talk. When you verbally agree with the talker, you cause the person to share even more.

One other thought about the listener. Some people say, "When I listen, it seems to cause the other person to just talk and talk and talk. Why?" Perhaps initially it does, but if you remain perfectly silent, you create such tension within the person speaking that the person begins to back off. By not responding, you let the other individual know that you are through with your part of the conversation. However, I am not advocating use of the silent treatment, that devastatingly unfair weapon that in time will erode a relationship.

Why Listen?   Why do you listen to other people? True, we have been taught to listen, told to listen, and admonished to listen, but why?

There are four basic reasons why we listen to other people:

1. To understand the other person.
2. To enjoy the other person.
3. To learn something from the one talking (such as learning his or her language!).
4. To give help, assistance, or comfort to the person.

The world is made up of many pseudolisteners who masquerade as the real product. But anyone who has not listened for the above reasons does not *really* listen.

Often when we listen, we have mixed motives. Our purpose is far from meeting the above criteria. We may also listen to:

Make people think that we are interested, so they will like us.
Determine whether we are being accepted or rejected.
Buy time to prepare our next comment.
Try to discover the other person's vulnerabilities.
See if we are producing the desired effect.
Sometimes we half-listen because we don't know how to get away without offending the person.

Hindrances to Listening

Have you ever traveled somewhere and suddenly come face-to-face with some hindrance in the road? All of a sudden you discovered that you were blocked from arriving at your destination. Likewise a number of hindrances to listening can prevent us from arriving at our destination. Here are some of them. Think of a time when you experienced one of these and try to remember why it occurred!

Do you ever *compare* yourself to the person speaking? Perhaps you've thought, *Oh, I could do that better; He thinks* he's *had it rough. He ought to hear* my *story; I'm more capable than he is.* When you are so busy measuring, you can't take much in! Think of a time when you might compare yourself as you listen to another person.

The most common hindrance is *rehearsing* what you're going to say. In fact, some people actually rehearse the entire conversation. We are most prone to do this when the other person says something we don't want to hear and we form our defense, or if the person's topic triggers a similar experience from our memory banks, and we want our opportunity to share it.

Defensiveness wipes out listening. We need to accept what the other person says without necessarily agreeing with it.

Frequently we become defensive because we fear criticism. As long as we remain this way, we cannot benefit from what the other person might say that could help us. The Book of Proverbs offers some guidelines on the subject:

> If you refuse criticism you will end in poverty and disgrace; if you accept criticism you are on the road to fame.
>
> Proverbs 13:18 TLB

> Don't refuse to accept criticism; get all the help you can.
>
> Proverbs 23:12 TLB

> It is a badge of honor to accept valid criticism.
>
> Proverbs 25:12 TLB

> A man who refuses to admit his mistakes can never be successful. But if he confesses and forsakes them, he gets another chance.
>
> Proverbs 28:13 TLB

Filtering is another term for *selective listening*. We filter when we avoid hearing something. It could be anything that is negative, threatening, critical, or unpleasant. The words do not register with us, and we can swear on a stack of Bibles that the other person never said what he says he did.

Attitudes or *biases* we hold toward other individuals block our listening. People who speak in a certain tone of voice, members of an ethnic group or of the opposite sex, people who remind us of someone from our past can all be part of the reason we don't hear what is being said. What type of person is hard for you to listen to, and why is that so? Some find it easier to listen to an angry person than a sarcastic one; certain gestures and phrases can also bother us *if we let them*. Some people are distracted in their listening because of the sex or occupation of the person speaking. Our expectations of what a man shares and doesn't share and what a woman should or should not share will also influence us.

We may listen more to those who:

Are in a position over us.
Are in a prestigious position.
Are in agreement with us.

Your *attitude toward life* will affect your listening. Some individuals listen with optimism and others with pessimism. Do you hear the good news or only the bad news? Both are there, but you may be selective in what you take in.

Mind reading is another great hindrance to true listening. In fact, mind reading can get us into trouble because we tend to believe what we *think* rather than what the other person *says*. In effect we end up calling the person a liar! We distrust what is verbally shared and try to figure out what the other person *really* thinks or means. Mind readers make assumptions: *He says he likes the dinner, but he's just being polite. He doesn't really care for it. I bet he really doesn't like what I just painted. He feels obligated.*

When you make an assumption, you have three choices:

You can give it up, check it out by asking a question, or give as much possibility to the opposite assumption as to the one you hold.

When you engage in selective listening, you also engage in selective retention. You remember certain comments and situations and forget those you reject. David Augsburger says, "Memory is the greatest editor of all, and it discards major pieces of information while treasuring trifles."[1]

Improve Your Listening Skills

We've seen how we tune out others. How can we tune them in instead? When you listen, one of the best ways to respond is by asking a question so you have more information upon which to decide whether what was said is true or not. "Could you tell me a bit more?" "Could you give me a specific example?" "What would you like me to do differently?" Or you might say, "Thank you for letting me know your perspective. I will think about it," or, "That's interesting. I hadn't considered it in that way. I'll have to think about that," or, "What you're saying may have some truth in it. Tell me some more." These statements can have a disarming effect upon the other person as well as giving you more information.

Would you like to improve your listening skills? Let me share a few general hints on how to polish your listening skills and overcome the hindrances to listening.

Listen in an Active Manner. Be alive when you listen, don't be a corpse. In active listening you participate by asking questions and giving feedback But the key is to do it in the other person's language! Notice how he or she talks. If he asks questions or gives feedback in an abbreviated form, do the same. If he gives detail and elaborates with descriptive words, do the same.

When you actively listen, you do three things: paraphrase, clarify, and give feedback.

Paraphrasing means you state in your own words what you believe the other person said. This helps you to understand

and know what the other person means. It also helps you cut through the hindrances to listening.

You may be thinking, *But I'm not a counselor. That's something they are trained to do.* However anyone can learn to actively listen. It's very easy. When you paraphrase, you use lead-ins such as:

"What I hear you saying is. . . ."
"Let me understand. What you were feeling was. . . ."
"If I hear you correctly, you're saying. . . ."
"Do you mean that . . . ?"

What happens when you do this? There are six specific benefits of paraphrasing:

1. The person speaking will appreciate feeling heard by you.
2. This technique lessens anger and brings a sense of calm to a heated discussion.
3. It eliminates miscommunication. Corrections are made on the spot.
4. You will remember what was said.
5. It is the best way to eliminate listening hindrances.
6. Emotionally you will be calmer and feel more in control during the interaction.

Clarifying often accompanies paraphrasing. It is very simple. You just ask questions until you fully understand what the other person means. This helps you hear specifics in the proper context. Clarifying also lets the other person know that you are with him and interested in what he is saying.

Feedback is sharing your thoughts and feelings in a non-judgmental way. Your feedback helps the other person understand the effect of his communication. During feedback apply these biblical principles that vitally build relationships.

"A word fitly spoken and in due season is like apples of gold in a setting of silver" (Proverbs 25:11 AMP).

"Gentle words cause life and health; griping brings discouragement. . . . Everyone enjoys giving good advice, and how wonderful it is to be able to say the right thing at the right time!"(Proverbs 15:4, 23 TLB).

"Speaking the truth in love . . ." (Ephesians 4:15). When we speak the truth in love our relationship is cemented together better than it was before. That takes sensitivity and perceptiveness.

Listen With Empathy.　　This means both caring and seeing the situation from the other person's perspective. You may not like or agree with what is being said, but as you listen you realize that if you were experiencing what this person is experiencing, if you were standing where he is standing, you would probably feel the same way. Romans 12:15 says we are to weep with those who weep and rejoice with those who rejoice. That is what empathy is all about.

Listen With Openness.　　Selective listening, defensive listening, and filtered listening do not denote open listening. Listening with openness means discovering how the other person's point of view makes sense to you. How do you do this? Someone has suggested that you listen as though you were an anthropologist and imagine that the other person is from another planet or country. His customs, beliefs, and way of thinking are different from yours. You as the anthropologist are trying to understand it all. This means you must listen to all that is being shared, *without* judgment.

Listening With Awareness.　　Be aware of what the other person says and how it compares with the facts. Be aware of whether or not the message of the other person is consistent. By being consistent I mean, do the words, tone, and body language match up? If you find a discrepancy between any of the three, you may not really know what the other person is saying. You'll find out more about this in the following chapters.

Listening is one of the greatest gifts you can give another person!

By listening, you can influence the conversation and have more impact than if you were talking!

By listening, you will be able to learn the other person's language and thus be able to communicate to the fullest!

By listening with your ears and your eyes, you will be a very perceptive listener.

Energy Builders

1. What facts did you learn about listening from this chapter? Have you experienced the truth of them in your life?

2. How have you been a good listener in the past? Where do you need to improve? What skills do you need to learn?

3. What are the four reasons for listening? Do you listen with them in mind? Have you often listened with mixed motives? Do you need to tune in to others better?

4. What are some of the hindrances to listening? Which ones have kept you from hearing what others say? What techniques can you use to combat these?

5. What will you do this week with the information in this chapter? Describe how your communication will be different.

Three

Listening With Your Eyes _____

My son Matthew taught me to listen with my eyes. I had no other option. Even today as he nears the age of twenty, my profoundly mentally retarded boy still knows just a few words, and even those have little or no meaning. But he is also a tremendous gift from God, because his presence has changed our lives. We have learned so much from him.

When Matthew lived at home, he couldn't communicate his needs. He would grab our hands and place them on his head or rub his head against us to show us that something was wrong. We learned to read his body movements and his eyes to detect any type of seizure activity. In time I found that I had also begun to listen to my clients with my eyes and hear what they could not put into words. I was becoming a total listener!

You can become a total listener as well.

Every now and then I run into a married couple who make an appointment for counseling and begin the session by saying, "Our problem is we don't communicate!" What they don't realize is that you cannot "not communicate" with others. Your feelings and attitudes are shared even without your saying a word. A person may lie verbally, but it is very difficult to tell a lie nonverbally. If you say you are happy or that nothing is wrong and you look downcast, what should we believe—what you say verbally or nonverbally?

Nonverbal Communication

You communicate nonverbally in two different ways. One is with your body movements, such as gestures, your posture, and your facial expression. The second way in which nonverbals communicate is in spatial relationship. How much distance you put between yourself and others conveys a definite message.

Did you know that your nonverbals make up 55 percent of your message when you are in face-to-face conversation with another person?

Are you familiar with the word *congruence?* It means "to agree or coincide." When you communicate nonverbally, there is usually a congruence to your verbals. They agree with one another. But the problem occurs when the words and the nonverbals seem to disagree. You might say, "I wish more people would talk to me. They seem to ignore me." But you sit on the edge of groups, slouch in your chair, fold your arms, and avoid eye contact. Your nonverbals say, "Ignore me."

In order to hear the message the other person sends you nonverbally, you need to listen with your eyes. Then you can make any adjustments needed in order to communicate better with that person. If someone nods her head while you talk to her, she could be saying, "I understand," "I agree," or, "Go on." If she raises her eyebrows, she could be saying, "I don't know about that," or, "I didn't know that." If she looks puzzled, perhaps you need to give more clarification.

Facial Expression

What do you say with your face? What do others say with their faces? Turn off the sound on the TV some evening and concentrate on the facial expressions of the performers. In fact if you have a VCR, record the program at the same time and watch it again, later, with sound, to see if your perception was accurate. Browse through some magazines and as you do so cover the people's bodies and just look at their faces. What does their facial expression say to you? What do they intend to say with their faces? The more of the face you cover, the more difficult you'll find it to read emotions and attitudes. Our faces are the most expressive parts of our bodies.

Sometimes we don't want our faces to express what we are saying, and we attempt to cover up our expressions. For example we may use our hands to cover our mouths when we tell a lie. Children, adolescents, and adults have their own variation of covering their lies. A child usually uses one or both hands to cover her mouth right after she has told a lie. A teenager brings his hands to his mouth, but instead of covering his mouth, he rubs his finger lightly around it. Adults refine the technique. An adult raises her hand to cover her mouth but often touches the bottom part of the nose instead of covering the mouth. In fact, the older a person gets, the more sophisticated and less obvious the gestures become, and the harder it is to read them.

Extremity Nonverbals

Our gestures send the sensitive listener messages. Some people talk with their hands a great deal. I happen to be one of those, and my daughter has often told me that if you were to tie my hands behind me, I wouldn't be able to talk. I don't think it would be that bad, but I do find myself gesturing even when I am talking on the telephone!

We scratch our heads when we are puzzled or touch our noses when we are in doubt. When we want to interrupt we often tug one ear. A frustrated or angry person often rubs his neck. Hands are used to convey grief by wringing of the hands. We also rub them in anticipation. What do the following nonverbals mean to you?

Clenched hands
Crossed arms
Hands on the knees when sitting
Hands on the hips
Hands behind the back
Hands locked behind the head
Hands in the pockets

Generally speaking, each of these nonverbals conveys a specific message, although there will be exceptions. Clenched hands can be a sign of anger or tension. What do you feel when you clench your hands? Hands on the hips can be a sign of impatience. How do *you* show impatience? Hands behind the back can mean the person is not in control of himself at that moment. Hands locked behind the head can indicate a statement of superiority. Some people put their hands in their pockets to hide their meaning. Crossed arms can indicate defensiveness, and arms extended out in front with palms up can mean sincerity! Isn't it amazing how much your body says about you, without your having to say a word?

Have you ever been in a meeting and become bored? Most of us have, but have you ever told the speaker you were bored? You probably think, *Are you kidding? That would be rude. There's no way I would ever do that.* Chances are, however, that all of us have conveyed our boredom to the speaker. How? Again, through body language. When a listener begins to use his hand to support his head, it signals that boredom is creeping in. The hand keeps the head up and in some cases keeps us from falling asleep. If the head is fully supported by the hand, the boredom is intense.

If someone drums her fingers or taps her feet while a person is speaking, it does not indicate boredom, but impatience. If the hand is on the cheek, either closed or with the index finger pointed upward, the person is evaluating what the speaker says.

Speaking of the head, watch the position of the listener's head. If the person's head is up, he or she has a neutral attitude about what is being heard. The head usually remains still, except for an occasional small nod. If the head tilts to one side, it indicates that interest has now developed. If you see someone tilt her head and lean forward with hand to chin, you are getting your point across. But when a person's head goes down, it can indicate that his attitude is negative and even judgmental. If you can't get his head up, you may end up with a communication problem!

Not only do your head and your hands communicate, but your feet and legs do as well. When you sit talking with someone and your legs are uncrossed and slightly apart, you communicate an attitude of openness. If you sit straddling a chair, you may send a message of dominance. If you sit with one leg over the arm of the chair, you pass on a message of indifference. Some people sit with one leg crossed over the other because it feels comfortable, and they have been doing it for years. Yet it could be a sign of boredom, anger, or frustration; it can indicate being closed to the other person's message to you at that time. When all the limbs are uncrossed, it conveys agreement. The direction of your arms and legs indicates the direction in which you feel the most interest.

You may be thinking, *I don't use my body much. And I certainly don't send all those messages.* May I suggest you try an experiment? Tell an experience or a story to someone, but purpose ahead of time not to shift your body or use any gestures whatsoever. This will take some intense concentration and effort. Several minutes into the story, begin using your body. After you have finished, analyze how you felt when you couldn't use any gestures. Ask the other person what she heard from you and how she felt when you were not using any gestures. Ask her what your gestures meant when you did use them.

The ideal experience would be to have someone else videotape you while you talk to a group or with another person. Watch the video without the sound first; then turn on the sound. What did you learn about yourself and the way you communicate?

Distance Nonverbals

We also communicate by the distance we stand or sit from another person. You've probably experienced the situation when you have had an argument with a family member and that person has moved and sat as far away from you as possible. Or a young couple in love has a spat, and she moves to the other side of the couch instead of sitting in his lap. These are quite obvious. Anthropologist Edward T. Hall describes four different zones people use when they interact with others. We use these unconsciously. Most of us don't think, "I need to stand two and one-half feet from this person and one and one-half feet from this one and stay eight feet from that individual," we just do what feels comfortable.

Intimate distance is quite close, usually six to eighteen inches from the other person's body. This is the distance used by close friends, those in love, and children hanging onto their friends or parents. Those who aren't intimate usually feel uncomfortable being this close to another person. Imagine yourself getting into a crowded elevator. Everyone there remains very conscious of not touching one another. Do the people in an elevator engage others in eye contact? Not usually. They avoid it. You have to stand at an intimate distance to get where you are going, but as soon as a few people leave the elevator, those remaining spread out. To shake people up, get into a crowded elevator sometime and don't turn around. Stand facing the crowd, and engage some of them in eye contact. You will really make them uncomfortable unless you relieve their anxiety with a statement like, "You've wondered why I've called you here today," or, "Is this the line to the men's room?"

Personal distance runs from one and one-half to two and one-half feet and is a very comfortable distance for conversation. You can talk to friends or strangers at this distance at a social gathering and feel at ease.

Several years ago at the seminary I teach at, I had a student who was raised in Chile. His parents were missionaries, and for most of his life he lived there. My first encounter with him felt a bit uncomfortable, since he came and stood very close to me. Unconsciously I began to put some distance between us by backing up a bit, but he moved closer. Finally he realized what was happening and shared with me that people in his country have different distances than we do here. There it is the custom to talk with someone at a very close distance. He also explained that he found most North Americans couldn't handle this, because of our training and culture. This is why many Latin people feel that Americans are standoffish, and some Americans feel that Latins are aggressive and pushy.

After this student told me that, I no longer backed off when we talked together. I understood that his personal zone was much closer, so I accepted his distance and became quite comfortable with it. The young man left school and went onto a church staff. I saw him several years later, and remembering his background, I went up and said hello and started to converse with him. I purposely stood very close to him, face-to-face, and noticed that he started to inch back a bit. Then he caught himself, and we both laughed. He had become Americanized, and I had threatened him with my Latin approach. Gradually he had accepted the American distance. Now both of us could shift either way, which gave us greater flexibility and comfort in talking.

Social distance is four to seven feet. We use this in talking with clients or perhaps someone trying to sell us something or fix something for us. Supervisors, managers, or company presidents use a greater distance to convey their position of importance. Often they will also sit, while the other person stands, to convey their position.

Public distance is twelve to twenty feet and is used for formal gatherings. Little intimacy is indicated at this distance.

Remember, these zones do vary from culture to culture and even from group to group. Dr. Hall's classifications are general, as well, and there will be many exceptions.

Yet the distance you place yourself from someone else does carry a message. Are you aware of the one you send or receive? Is your distance consistent with the relationship? Watch! Listen with your eyes!

Remember:

"The hearing ear and the seeing eye, the Lord has made both of them" (Proverbs 20:12).

Speak my language and I will respond to you.

Listening is one of the greatest gifts you can give to another person.

The person listening has more power or control over a conversation than the person speaking.

Become a total listener by listening with your eyes as well as your ears. Watch the person's face, arms, hands, and head. Watch your distance! It, too, conveys a message!

Energy Builders

1. How can you listen with your eyes? Have you ever closed your eyes and listened to a person talk? Did you understand him as well as you would have if you had watched his facial features and body motion?

2. What are some of the nonverbal clues a speaker can give you? Name some ways a person can indicate that her words do not really say what she feels. How can she express boredom? Anger? Puzzlement?

3. Have you ever felt uncomfortable about your spatial re-

lationship with another person? If so, why? Who do you feel comfortable with at an intimate distance? Personal distance? Social distance? How do you react if the distance feels wrong to you?

4. What will you do this week with the information in this chapter? Describe how your communication will be different.

Four

What Are You Trying to Say? How Do You Say It?

You're at a social gathering with a group of friends, and you are listening to a newcomer talk on and on. During a lull in the conversation, two of you excuse yourselves, and as you walk away you say, "Did you understand what he was trying to say?" Your friend replies with a laugh, "No. I'm not even sure that *he* knew what he was trying to say!"

An uncommon occurrence? No! Many people talk without knowing for sure what they want to get across. Their purpose is clouded, and their presentation leaves the listener confused and perplexed. I've experienced both sides of this problem. On occasion I have wondered what the other individual or speaker is trying to get across, and other times I have caused others to wonder what I really wanted to say.

Rules for Clear Communication

Following a few basic communication principles, however, will enable us to be clear, consistent communicators.

1. Know When Something Needs to Be Said and Say It Straight. This means you do not assume that other people know what you think, feel, want, or need. They are not mind readers. Communication should be clear and direct. If anything, assume that the other person knows very little about what you are going to say and that you need to make it clear. None of us can attend a school for mind reading. We are all failures at being clairvoyant. I have heard people say, "We've been married for twenty years. Why should I have to tell her . . . ?" "He should know how much that hurt. . . ." Or, "It was so obvious. Why should anyone have to express it?" Obvious to whom? Clearly not to the other party.

Communicating directly means you don't make assumptions, you don't hint, you are not devious, you do not go through other people in order to share your message. All these approaches lead to distortions. One of my favorite examples is of the woman who tried to get her point across to her husband by making sweeping generalizations about what "everyone" thought or felt. Her husband stayed out late quite often, and she felt irritated. But she did not want to be that direct about her emotions.

One day she said, "Some wives would be angry at your staying out so late at night."

"You mad or something?" he asked.

"Oh, no. *I'm* not," she said. "But *some* wives would be."

This woman put herself in a position of denying her own thoughts, feelings, and intentions. When you *are* direct, you speak the truth by stating your real needs and feelings. When you ask questions, you ask truthful ones. How can questions be falsehoods? Easily. If you ask a question, desiring only one type of response, that becomes a setup! When you ask, the other person should have the freedom to give his or her own honest answer, no matter how you respond. If you don't want to hear an answer, don't ask the question!

If you feel angry about something, you don't say you are tired. If you don't want to go to a social gathering, you say so instead of saying, "Oh, I don't know. I guess I could go for a while. . . ." By not being completely open, we create false impressions, find that our needs are not being met, perhaps protect ourselves, but in the long run create distance between ourselves and other people.

When I am confused about a person's message to me, I now reply, "What are you saying? I would like to be sure I understand you." This puts more responsibility on the person to clarify. Sometimes I have to repeat this two or three times to draw out the real intent. Creating an atmosphere of comfort that will assist the other person to share is one of the listener's important roles.

QUESTION: Why am I saying this? What do I want to say? What do I want the other person to hear?

2. Be Aware of the Importance of Timing. Proverbs 15:23 (AMP) says, "A word spoken at the right moment, how good it is!" Most emotions should be shared at the moment you experience them, because delaying distorts them. When you respond immediately, it allows the other individual to learn what you feel and what you need. For example, in a conversation what is important to you may not seem significant to the other person. Therefore, delaying your response may allow the person to totally forget what he or she said! Then that person wonders what you are talking about when you bring it up later, and you wonder why the person is so insensitive in not remembering!

We also need to give an immediate response to minimize our own distortion. *What do you mean my own distortion? I don't distort!* you may be thinking or feeling. Most of us are not aware of how we distort messages, but we all do it sometimes. Why do we distort? *Because what we see and what we hear are often confused or affected by what we think and feel!*

That's right. The feelings we experience as well as our immediate or even previous thoughts can distort what we take in through our eyes and ears. To avoid confusion, I now ask myself, *What have I been thinking about this person or situation? Are my thoughts valid at this time? What am I feeling right now?* By asking myself these questions while we are still communicating, I give myself the opportunity to clarify the other person's point of view. Maybe I need to ask the person a question or share what he did again. At the same time as I use immediate response, I also delay my own reaction long enough to help me truly capture the meaning that person wants to get across.

> QUESTION: What static interferes with your communication? Your feelings, thoughts, physical state, and so on? Discover this and take corrective action and your communication will improve!

3. Know Exactly What You Are Going to Say and Say It. When you talk with another person, do you want to share your *feelings, needs, thoughts,* or *observations?* Or do you share all four? Sometimes we blend and run these together so much that we lose all clarity.

When you share a thought, you offer another person your conclusions, your observations, your value judgments, or beliefs and opinions. How do you state these? In such a way that others understand, want to continue listening, are interested? Do you ever indicate that what you are sharing is a thought, compared to a feeling?

When you share an observation, you talk like a scientist or a police detective or even a refrigerator repairman. There are no speculations or conclusions. You share the facts! "I have lived in Long Beach for eighteen years" is a strictly factual observation. "I think I might end up living here for another ten years, if plans continue as they are" is a thought based on some data I haven't yet shared with you.

Thoughts and conclusions are relatively easy to share. Feelings are more difficult. Why? Because our feelings may be a threat. The other person may not want to hear about my anger, grief, depression, sorrow, or elation. Many people do not understand feelings, so from their point of view I would be speaking a foreign language. In fact, some people in our society have been raised emotionally handicapped! They have no feeling awareness and no vocabulary for expressing feelings. But if you ever want true and deep intimacy to occur in a relationship, you *must* share your emotions. Yes, feeling statements are risky, but the potential rewards are worthwhile. Really it is quite easy to express them.

Verbally, you can describe your feelings four ways:

1. Identify or name the feeling. "I feel angry." "I feel sad." "I feel good about you."

2. Use similies and metaphors. We do not always have enough labels to describe our emotions, so we sometimes invent similies and metaphors to describe feelings. "I felt like a cool breeze blowing through the air." "I felt so bad, you'd think a herd of elephants had run over me during the night."

3. Report the time of response or the action your feelings urge you to do. "Right then I felt like hugging you." "I was so upset I felt like dumping my dinner plate in your lap that night."

4. Use figures of speech, such as "The sun is smiling on me today." "I felt as if a dark cloud were following me around yesterday."

How do you share your needs? Do you do it consciously? You alone can tell what you need and want and communicate that to others. In order for them to know, they must hear about it. People are not clairvoyant! If you believe they are, get ready to become disappointed and angry! When you feel they should be, if you decide to share your need, it will probably come across as a demand, which people will resist. Instead express your needs in a pleasant tone of voice, with clarity, and without blame or judgment. Needs are just simple requests of what would help or please you.

Whether you share a need, feeling, observation, or thought, people may wonder what your purpose is and what you intend. Let them know your *intentions*, and your communication will begin to bring results.

Wife: "I want very much to end this argument, honey."

Husband: "I didn't know that. I thought you were too upset to stop. Sounds good to me—I'd like to come to some conclusion, too."

Document what you say with facts, or if you are making an observation about another person, use some descriptive behavioral data.

"I think you're elated. I see a smile on your face, and your voice sounds up, to me."

"I wonder if you feel all right. You seem to be moving more slowly today. You look kind of down in the mouth, and your voice seems kind of flat. Do you think you could be catching the flu?"

"Your tone of voice makes me feel you are upset over something. What's on your mind?"

"I'm kind of concerned. You're frowning, and I'm not sure what that means. Don't you understand, or do you disagree? It would help me if you could tell me what your frown means."

By knowing what you are going to say and saying it, you will avoid a communication booby trap! When you are not in tune with your own words, you tend to give partial messages. That's a booby trap because it creates a false impression for the listener. The authors of the book *Messages* talk about how important it is to stay in tune and send whole messages.

Whole messages include all four kinds of expressions: what you see, think, feel, and need. Intimate relationships thrive on whole messages. Your closest friends, your mate, and your family can't know the real you unless you share all your experiences. That means not leaving things out, not covering up your anger, not squelching your wants. It means giving accurate feedback about what you observe, clearly stating your inferences and conclusions, saying how it all makes you feel, and if you need something or see possibilities for change, making straight-forward requests or suggestions.

When you leave something out, it's called a partial message. Partial messages create confusion and mistrust. People sense something is missing, but they don't know what. They're turned off when they hear judgments untempered by your feelings and hopes. They resist hearing anger that doesn't include the story of your frustration or hurt. They are uncomfortable with demands growing from unexpressed feelings and assumptions.[1]

Of course in some situations you do not express all four, but your communication still works effectively. You do not share whole messages with your gas-station attendant or grocery-store clerk. Often as we talk with friends, some conversations are just informational. But if we leave out some part that is significant, we have only partially communicated.

QUESTIONS: When you share, are you sharing what is an actual fact based upon what you know from reading, hearing, or observing?
Have you labeled and identified your conclusions?
Have you expressed your feelings in a way that others can understand and accept them?
Do you share your needs as requests and not demands?
Are you giving whole or partial messages?

You may be thinking communication is a lot of work. Yes and no! Yes, at first, until these principles become a normal pattern for you, but as your sensitivity develops, it becomes easier and easier.

Communication Beyond Words

So far I have talked about stating clearly what you want and intend to say at the proper time. Now I would like to consider the elements that make up your *paralanguage!* When you talk with a friend, a fellow employee, or a family member, you really don't depend upon words alone to make your point. You actually depend more upon the vocal component of your communication. It includes your pitch, the raising or lowering of your voice. It also includes resonance. For the past two years I have been taking trumpet lessons from an excellent young teacher. He keeps after me to "make the sound rich! Make it ring!" Now and then it does, and I feel great when that happens. My teacher is talking about resonance. In speech it refers to the richness or thinness of our voices. They can be thin and high or deep and full. With practice you can control both pitch and resonance.

Paralanguage includes your articulation—how you enunciate your words. You can become so relaxed in your conversation that some of your words slur, or you may speak so precisely that each word sounds as if it has been bitten off and shot out of a gun.

The tempo or the speed of your words also forms part of your paralanguage. This factor reflects your attitudes and emotions. Remember a time when you heard someone talking fast? What message did he convey? Often it is excitement. Such people can be quite persuasive, but if their speech becomes *too* rapid we may start feeling a bit uneasy. In a normal conversation, talking too fast may be a sign of insecurity. On the other hand, a person who talks very slowly and deliberately may reflect either indifference or cultural upbringing. People raised in the country tend to talk more slowly than those from the large cities.

Volume is another element in paralanguage. Loudness may reflect enthusiasm and confidence, aggressiveness, or as in some speeches and sermons, it can indicate the speaker has a weak point in his presentation and wants to hide it by speaking more loudly. A soft voice can convey caring, understanding, empathy, intimacy, or a lack of confidence.

Finally, rhythm emphasizes certain words in a sentence. If I asked, "Are you going out tonight?" that is a simple question because all the words are alike. But note what happens when I change emphasis, "Are *you* going out tonight?" or, "Are *you* going out *tonight?*" If my secretary comes in late and apologizes and I say, "Oh, that's all right, it's only nine-thirty," my response seems reasonable and straightforward. But if I change just one word, I change the meaning and reveal much more about my emotions. "It's *only* nine-thirty" has a different message. If you say to me after I've made a request, "Wait just a minute," and give equal emphasis to every word, you make a request. But if the word *just* or *minute* is emphasized, you could be conveying irritation or annoyance.

We don't often use just one element of paralanguage by itself but blend them to convey many varied meanings.

I listen more for paralanguage than actual words, and I hope you do, too. Why? Because through this people share their moods and attitudes. In this manner more is revealed about a person and what he feels than by his words alone. As you watch a film or TV program, close your eyes and listen for the pitch, resonance, articulation, tempo, volume, and rhythm. The message is there. What does it say to you?

Have you watched some of the current movies that have talking robots? Their speech is monotonous, because it doesn't change. A few people talk in the same way. They don't vary their pitch, resonance, volume, tempo, or rhythm. When we hear them, we wonder, *Are they bored with life or themselves or what?* You see, your paralanguage often reflects your personality! It tells others who you are and even what you have to offer.

Over the past several years, I have suggested the following exercise to hundreds of people. Tape record your family conversation around the dinner table for a week and then listen to the conversations. The value is tremendous. You not only have the opportunity to hear the interaction between family members, the words used, the interruptions, but you start to become conscious of your paralanguage.[2]

Is your voice reflecting what you want to say? Are your words consistent with your voice? What do you like about your voice? What do you dislike?

Now let's put these first four chapters together. What have I said and what have you heard? Let's check it out:

Speak the other person's language.

Listening is one of the greatest gifts you can give another person.

By listening, you will be able to learn the other person's language.

Become a total listener by listening with your eyes as well as with your ears.

Be aware of what you want to say and how you sound. Remember that what you see and what you hear is often confused or affected by what you think and feel inside.

Share whole messages to avoid communication booby traps.

Listen for your own and other people's paralanguage. Feelings and attitudes are shared in this manner.

Energy Builders

1. What are the rules for clear communication? How have you already used them in your communication? What ones do you need to build skill in?

2. How can feelings complicate communication? When you communicate, do you share feelings, needs, thoughts, or observations? How does that influence the way you communicate? The way others understand you?

3. Have you given partial messages to others? When? Have you given partial messages when you should have given whole ones? What happened? Have you received partial messages from others? What would have helped you understand them better?

4. What does it mean to have communication beyond words? What is paralanguage? Describe your own paralanguage: How do you enunciate your words? At what tempo do you speak? How loud is your normal speaking voice? Is it easy for you to vary these? Have others ever commented on them?

5. What will you do this week with the information in this chapter? Describe how your communication will be different.

Five

Speak the Other Person's Language _____

One Tuesday afternoon I waited for my next clients, a young couple I had never met who were coming in for their first session of premarital counseling. I looked forward to the challenge of working with them, because I believe very strongly in the effectiveness and value of premarital preparation. As I walked through the waiting room, a new therapist on my staff stopped me and said, "Norm, I see you have a new couple coming in at two o'clock, and they're coming for premarital. I've never had the chance to conduct premarital yet, nor do I have much background in it from my schooling. What do you try to accomplish in the first session?"

At first I thought of sharing the eight topics I try to cover, but then I decided upon a different approach. "You know, John," I replied, "it doesn't really matter whether I am seeing an individual, a married couple, or an engaged couple. In the first session, among other things, I try to learn their language and speak it. Once I do that, we're on our way. Well, here they are. I'll see you later, John."

As I turned to greet the couple and lead them into my office, John stood there with a quizzical look on his face, mulling over what he had just heard.

Establishing Communication

After the preliminary introductions, Jan, Bill, and I plunged into our topics. This young, alert, and eager couple wanted to build a marriage that would last, that would be fulfilling for both of them, and that would reflect their Christian commitment.

About halfway into the session, I paused, looked at them, and told them, "I think it's about time to drop a time bomb on you, before we go any further." I paused, noticing that I definitely had their attention. They glanced at each other, then back at me. I continued, "I would be remiss if I didn't share this with you early in our time together. The person seated across from you—the one you're about to marry. Look at that individual right now, please." They turned and looked at each other, with puzzled expressions.

"I just want you to remember," I continued, "that person is a foreigner. You are going to be marrying a foreigner!"

I paused and let my statements sink in. They looked at me, then back at each other. Jan raised her eyebrows as she faced Bill. Bill turned to me and said, "What are you talking about, marrying a foreigner?"

I replied, "Yes, you are going to be marrying a foreigner. That's all."

Bill looked back at Jan and then at me. "What do you

mean marry a foreigner? We're both from this country." His voice took on a staccato beat. "In fact, we couldn't be better matched or more alike! We were both born and raised in California; we're both white; our parents were born and raised in this country, and so were their parents. How are we foreigners?"

I laughed a bit and said, "Well, this comes as a shock to most couples, and I do share this with almost everyone I work with now. You and Jan *are* similar. But you were both raised in different homes with different parents, siblings, experiences, and in effect a different culture. You may eat the same types of foods, but they were prepared differently. You have different customs, different rituals in your families, different beliefs and values, and you each learned a different language. If you want to have the kind of marriage you have described to me, your biggest task is going to be to learn about the other person's culture, to develop the flexibility to be comfortable with either set of customs, and above all, to learn your partner's language so that you can speak it!"

Jan said softly, "You mean, Bill and I, even though we've gone together for three years, still need to learn more about communication and how we talk with each other. Hmmm. You know, I *have* felt that way at times. On occasion I've sensed that Bill and I were sort of out of touch with each other, even though we had done a lot of talking and sharing. We would talk and talk, and at the time we each seemed to grasp what the other person was sharing, but later it felt as if we hadn't talked at all. He didn't catch what I had said. Other times he has a difficult time understanding me. And I don't understand why."

"Jan," I said, "right now you're sensing and sharing something many individuals feel perplexed about for many years of their marriage. Bill, what do you think about this?"

Bill smiled slightly. "Yes, I see what you're getting at now. Jan and I do talk quite a bit, but sometimes I wonder why she doesn't understand my perspective. I state my point of view, but from the questions she asks, it's as though she'd never heard me. So I try to explain again. In fact, at times I think we *over*talk about some things. I like to make everything clear and simple and to the point, but we tend to go on and—"

Jan interrupted, "Bill, the reason we go on and on at times is because you don't seem to understand what *I'm* feeling. I need to make sure that I'm understood by you, so we don't have misunderstandings."

"Jan," I said, "it's important to you that Bill understands your feelings, right? Bill, you want Jan to understand your perspective and view it your way, right?" They both nodded. "Could it be that some of the words you use aren't in the other person's vocabulary? Could it be that in some way you're not speaking the other person's language?"

Jan replied first. "Perhaps that's what's happening." She thought for a minute and then continued softly, "Now that we are talking about this, I've become aware of something else. I feel we've made more progress, but at first we had to work on how we shared with each other. I didn't understand what was going on, until I went to Bill's home for dinner the first time. What a shock!"

Bill laughed in instant recognition. "Yes, it was a shock for her."

"What happened?" I asked.

Jan replied, "We went to his home and had dinner with his parents and two brothers and sister. Naturally, I felt a bit apprehensive, since I wanted to make a good impression. I felt a little on edge, and when I do, I tend to quiet down somewhat. Not that I don't talk as much as I usually do, but I get more hesitant and soft-spoken.Once we got into dinner, I'm afraid I sat there with my mouth open in shock—at least I felt as if I did. Bill's family is totally different from mine. My family is polite and quiet, and they rarely raise their voices. If they do, *watch out!* It means that someone is angry, but that doesn't happen often.

"But Bill and his family," she continued, "they raise their voices, interrupt, carry on two or three conversations at once, even shout at times! I was numb by the time dinner was over and felt very uncomfortable. When we left, the first thing I said to Bill was, 'Bill, your family is such an angry group of people—and they didn't seem very polite toward one another, either. They interrupted and didn't let people finish.' "

At this point Bill animatedly picked up the story. "That came as a big surprise to me! 'What do you mean? My family loves each other! They're very close-knit and loyal,' I told her. 'In fact, they were just themselves tonight, which is good. That means they liked you and looked at you as someone they could be themselves with. Nobody was angry. That's just the way we talk! We've always been that way, and so are my grandparents and aunts and uncles and their families! We're just loud and have our own style of communicating. I'm that way, too.' "

"It was a shock for a while," Jan said. "The more I went with Bill, the more I discovered that he communicated that way. When he first raised his voice, I froze, because I thought he was angry, but I have since learned that he does that when he is excited and wants to emphasize something."

"So when you first went to Bill's home," I said quietly to Jan, "it was like entering another country, since they did things differently and in a sense spoke a different language. At first you felt a bit awkward, until you began to translate what they were saying into your own language. Am I right?"

They both laughed. "You're right," Bill replied. "Nobody ever put it that way before, but I can sure see how the idea of speaking another person's language makes sense."

"This picture of marrying a foreigner is clearing up a bit for you then, isn't it?" I asked.

"Oh, yeah," Bill replied. "In fact, I can see how both of us have already started to learn each other's family language and to adapt to each family."

"How?"

"Well," Bill continued, "after some time I noticed that Jan started to open up when we were with my family. She actually raised her voice and even interrupted at times. She really has learned to become one of us. I don't even think she was aware of the changes."

Jan spoke up. "Bill's right. I didn't think about how I was gradually changing, until one Christmas we had a tape recorder on during the family meal—or celebration as they call it. We sat and listened to it after dinner, and I was amazed when I heard myself. I sounded like them!"

"How did that feel to you, changing your way of communicating?"

"It was very comfortable," Jan answered me. "I enjoyed myself and I was getting closer to Bill's family as well. I felt good about this new relationship with his family."

"Bill, did you adapt to Jan's family?"

"I sure did," he told me. "In fact, the first time I was with them I felt really uncomfortable. I didn't know if they liked me or not. They were so polite and soft-spoken. I notice now that when we're with Jan's family I'm comfortable, but I don't talk as loudly with them as with my own family. Her family doesn't talk all that much, but they have as much fun as my family. I've learned that's okay."

"Bill," I asked, "do you and your family understand one another when you talk? Do you grasp what each person is saying?"

"Oh, sure," he replied, "we make sense to each other."

Then I asked Jan, "Do you and your family understand each other when you share together? Are you in touch with each other?"

"Oh, yes," Jan said, "we always are. I get along especially well with Mom. Dad, I must admit, doesn't always say too much. I wish he would. He's short and to the point with *very* little detail. At times I feel we have to drag any information out of him. When he does talk, he sounds like a newspaper reporter giving a condensed version of the daily news. He just gives the facts. And feelings! I don't know when I've heard Dad share his feelings. That's frustrated Mom over the years, too. But Mom and I really click."

Understanding Each Other

I turned the conversation back to the communication between this young couple. "Bill," I said, "you and your family seem to focus in well together as you talk, and Jan, you feel good about your communication with your mom. Now, what about the two of you together? What will it take for you two to communicate so that you understand each other?"

They looked at each other and then back at me. I waited and then said, "It's something to think about." I turned to Bill and, speeding up my rate of speech, asked, "By the way, Bill, are you and I communicating? Do you think we see eye to eye? Do we understand each other?"

Bill replied, "Oh, yes. You seem to see what I'm talking about, and I am getting the picture of this whole discussion of marrying a foreigner. I wonder, though, if I don't need a passport to marry Jan!"

We all laughed, and I turned to Jan and said softly, "How do you feel about our communication? Does it make sense?"

"Very much so," Jan answered. "You seem to have a handle on what I'm feeling, and what you say registers. We seem to speak the same language."

"Good," I said. "It's important that we learn not only to speak the same language but also to make sure we mean the same thing with our words. I have run into so many couples who get irritated and upset in their marriages because of such a simple matter as having different definitions for their words. You know, two people can speak Spanish and not mean the same thing. Two people can speak German and not mean the same thing. We're sitting here speaking English and using some of the same words, but we might have different meanings for them. Your experiences in life, your mindset, what you intend can give meaning to your words. My wife might ask, 'Could we stop at the store for a minute on our way home, Norm? I'll just be a minute.' I might take the word *minute* literally, but I had better not, because years of experience have taught me we're talking about fifteen to twenty minutes." Jan and Bill grinned and nodded their heads.

"Bill, has Jan ever said to you, 'Bill, could I talk to you for a minute about something?' and you said yes, assuming she meant a minute, but you're still discussing the issue thirty minutes later?" They both looked amazed, and Bill spoke up quickly.

"Tuesday night. That very thing happened Tuesday night. Jan wondered why I was getting uptight."

Jan broke in with, "Well, it was important. Did it matter how long it went on? You agreed we needed to talk about it, and I had felt that way for some time."

Bill responded, "Oh, no, it was all right. I just figured it'd be short, since you said *a minute*."

Jan replied with a bit more feeling, "But many times I feel *you* have set a time limit on our conversations. I almost sense that you're impatient and want to get to the bottom line. You don't want to hear all my reasons or feelings. In fact, I wish *you* would share more details with me. I wear a new outfit and ask you how it looks, and all you say is, 'It looks fine.' Can't you tell me any more about how you feel about it?"

Bill looked at me and rolled his eyes upward and then turned to Jan and said loudly, "But I said it looked fine. What else do you want to hear?"

I interrupted Bill and said, "On a scale of zero to ten with zero meaning it looks terrible—like it's out of the rag pile— and a ten meaning it's super—it's outstanding—where does the word *fine* fall?"

Bill said, "Oh, it's somewhere between an eight and a ten."

Jan looked surprised and blurted out, "How would I know that? That's the first I've heard that *fine* had any meaning at all!"

"This is what I mean," I interrupted, "when I say you need to define your words. Bill, if you couldn't use the word *fine* and had to give a three-line description of the dress Jan is wearing, what would you say?"

Bill thought a few seconds and then said, "Well, I like it.

The color looks good. The dress looks like you, and I like some of the detail around the waist. It fits well and I like the curves. It just seems to look like you. And the style is flashy."

I turned to Jan, "How do you feel about Bill's response?"

She smiled. "That really feels good. He really seemed to notice, and I enjoyed hearing his description."

Bill jumped in and said,"Well, I could do that, but when I'm with some of my other friends and we say *fine*, we know what we mean."

"I can understand that, Bill," I countered. "When you're with them you speak the same language, but when you're with Jan, you need to speak *her* language. She wants more detail, more description, more adjectives. That's what registers with her. This is a good example of what I mean by speaking the other person's language. Now that we're talking about it, which one of you tends to give more detail when you talk?" I looked back and forth between Bill and Jan and both of them pointed at Jan and laughed.

"I'm the detail person," Jan said. "Quite often Bill asks me to get to the point and give him the bottom line so he understands what I'm talking about. I just want to make sure that he's going to grasp what I'm sharing. I've always given a lot of detail and feelings, but sometimes it's as if he doesn't hear my feelings. He ignores them."

Bill replied, "I don't ignore what you are saying. I do see what you are getting at, but I don't always know what to do with those feelings. It's not that I always mind the detail, but I wish you would focus on the bottom line first, instead of going around the barn several times and then telling me what you're talking about. I like it straightforward and to the point."

I said, "Bill, you want Jan to communicate with you like a newspaper article."

"A newspaper article? How's that?" Bill asked.

"Most newspaper articles are structured like a pyramid," I continued. "The first sentence is a complete summary statement of what is in the article. Next comes a brief paragraph with some of the most significant summary items expanded.

The final larger portion of the article will contain the minute details."

"That's it," Bill said. "An approach like that makes sense to me. I can follow what's going on a lot better, and," he turned to Jan, "I would be willing to hear some more of the detail. But I don't think I need to hear as much detail as you enjoy hearing. I don't want a two-line news summary of what you say, but a *Reader's Digest* condensation would be helpful." They laughed together.

"Bill,' I said, "you're asking Jan to condense some of the details a bit and identify the bottom line right at the start. That helps you focus on her conversation better. Is that accurate?" He nodded. "That also means, Bill, since Jan enjoys detail, that when you share with her, you will give her more detail than you do now." Bill nodded.

"Now, does my statement about marrying a foreigner make more sense to you?" They both smiled and said, "Yes, definitely!"

"Once again let me go back to the question I asked a few minutes ago. Jan and Bill, what is it going to take, in addition to what we have already pointed out, for the two of you to understand each other and no longer be foreigners? What do you think, Bill? What do you feel, Jan?"

What do you as the reader feel? What are your thoughts about what needs to happen? What did you hear as you read through this account of Bill and Jan?

Now, before you read on, go back and read the interaction again. I did point out some steps for Jan and Bill to take, but I have not yet commented upon a key principle. Read it again and listen to their conversation. See if you can grasp this principle. Which person did you respond to more easily or understand more clearly? Did one more than the other speak your language? What did I do as I interacted with Jan and Bill?

Energy Builders

1. Have you ever felt as if someone close to you were speaking a foreign language, even though you could under-

stand all the words? Have you felt as if you were married to a foreigner? How have you been out of touch with each other? Why have you seen things differently? What did it take to hear each other clearly?

2. Have you ever had your words misunderstood by someone else because the two of you had slightly different meanings for the same word? How did it confuse your communication?

3. What kind of information do you want out of a conversation? Do you like to hear the bottom line first, or do you want to hear all the details? How do you speak to others? Do you need to change your style when you talk to some people you see often?

4. What will you do this week with the information in this chapter? Describe how your communication will be different.

Six

Learning Another Person's Language _____

Jan and Bill—a couple very similar to most in that their communication styles and patterns differ from each other—are on the edge of a major breakthrough. As they continued their premarital sessions they soon learned flexibility, which enabled them to speak each other's language. This prompted them to begin thinking, *If this is so effective in marital relationships, wouldn't it be effective in work and social relationships as well?* They discovered a major truth with that question! Speaking a person's language is not limited to marriage or courtship relationships. Actually I learned it by trial and error in the counseling office over the years and decided if it works so well there, it must work in other places as well, and it does.

I will never forget the couple who really introduced me to this study of communication. Tony and Mary were a young Italian couple whom I saw when I had my office in my home years ago. To be quite honest, after the first two sessions of counseling, I was totally frustrated with them. I had gotten nowhere. I attempted to be calm and rational and polite, while they interrupted me as well as each other. They shouted, attempted to outtalk each other, and as far as I could see, followed no known rules of communication.

Learn the Other Person's Rules of Communication

One Wednesday morning, I looked at my schedule and noticed that Tony and Mary were coming that afternoon. I thought, *Oh, no. Here goes another experience in futility and frustration. They don't listen to a thing I say, and they don't seem to listen to each other either. Boy! Well, if you can't beat them, why not join them? Hmm . . . , why not?* I decided to do just that.

When our session started, it soon evolved into two people talking at once, louder and louder, until I leaned forward, put out my hand toward Tony with a stopping action and said quite loudly, "Tony! Tony! Listen to Mary. She's got something to say. Mary, go ahead and talk. Tony will listen." Back and forth we went during the session. I felt like an orchestra conductor giving cues, raising or lowering the volume and pitch, controlling who was talking, and sometimes letting all three of us talk at once. I even outshouted them on occasion to get their attention! When the session ended, they thanked me and said, "Boy, was that a good session, Norm. See you next week."

I came out of the front room, through the soundproof door, into the kitchen. My wife looked around the corner from the family room, about fifty feet away, and said in a quiet voice, "Are you all right?"

I said, "Well, yes, why?"

"It sounded like World War Three in there," she replied. "I thought people were going to start throwing things. Who was so angry?"

"No one was angry," I said. "We were just loud. That's the way they talk, and the only way they listen to me is if I become like them." From that point on we had some loud and wild sessions, and I enjoyed myself thoroughly! Instead of expecting them to adapt to my style, I adapted to theirs, and they became willing to listen to me and the suggestions I eventually made. Tony and Mary taught me so much.

Develop Rapport

We use the word *rapport* when we talk about establishing relationships with other people, and in the field of counseling, psychologists are encouraged to establish rapport with the client as soon as possible. *Rapport* has been defined as "a relationship marked by harmony, conformity, accord, or affinity." It reflects a relationship that has agreement or even likeness or similarity.

No matter whom you meet in life, you will find that you have both differences with and similarities to that individual. Which do you emphasize? If you choose to emphasize your differences, you'll find it more difficult to establish rapport. If you emphasize what you have in common, you will be drawn closer more quickly. Look for your common ground.

People tend to like people who are like themselves. As one man put it, "Hey, it was great to go into that large group and discover several people who belonged to the same business club and read the same journals that I do. We hit it off right away, and I even have two invitations to dinner and racquetball!" We enjoy communicating with those who are like us, who have the same beliefs, values, hobbies, likes, and dislikes. How do you choose your friends? Do you select those who are totally different from you, with not one area of common ground? Not usually. We choose our friends from a pool of people who help us feel comfortable with ourselves and someone who is like us does that best. Perhaps this works as a subtle way of saying to ourselves that we are all right because there are others like us around.

How far does establishing rapport actually go? Do we have to become so much like others that we become clones? That we begin to lose our own identities? Not at all. You will still be who you are and reflect your own unique mannerisms and patterns of speech. However, by emphasizing similarities, you will be able to respond to a much greater variety of people socially and in your business world. In order to establish rapport, you have to take the opportunity to learn to be quite flexible. In fact, no doubt you already unconsciously do a lot of what I will suggest. Here I want only to identify it, refine it, and explain it for you so that you can become an even better communicator.

Mirror the Other Person's Behavior

Some of the outstanding therapists of our time are very adept at establishing rapport quickly. In watching them you discover that part of their process of developing rapport relies on mirroring. *Mirroring* simply means "giving back to the person portions of his or her own *nonverbal* behavior just as though the person were looking in a mirror."

We all do this to some degree. You go to a dinner party, and you find yourself matching your table manners and body postures to the expected level of informality or formality you feel is needed for that group. When I conduct seminars in different parts of the country, I think in advance which clothes would be most appropriate. I don't want to overdress or underdress, compared to the group who will be there. I find that on the East Coast the dress code is a bit more formal than in the Southwest.

Mirroring does not mean mimicking. From early childhood we have been taught that mimicking is not acceptable. Again and again we have heard, "Don't be a copycat," and we react negatively to such behavior. We have come to believe that mimicking is the same as making fun of a person, but actually mimicry is usually characterized by some exaggeration of a behavior or speech trait.

In contrast, mirroring occurs when you become sensitive to portions of your own behavior and response and to the other individual. What do you begin to become aware of? Portions of the other person's body posture, specific gestures, facial expressions, voice tone, tempo, and intonation patterns? In some cases I have seen the therapist match the person's breathing rhythms. But remember that these are very slight and subtle responses. If the person you talk with begins hitting himself on the side of the face every so often, don't do likewise. If the other individual comes running up after jogging four miles and is out of breath and panting, I would not encourage you to mirror this behavior.

I'd suggest a *subtle* matching of slight behaviors, mannerisms, and voice. For this to be effective you don't have to be a therapist. Friends talking together, a teacher with a student, two business associates—anyone can do it. Unconsciously (and now more consciously) I have done it in conversations with people in social situations as well as in the counseling office. A slight shifting of the body in order to sit in a fashion similar to the other person's, using a slight hand gesture that reflects one of his, pausing in much the same way she does are all examples of mirroring. Be aware of what you do when you are with other people. Watch their interactions as they communicate. Notice the quality of the interaction when mirroring is there and when it isn't. It goes on all around us every day.

Let's go back to Jan and Bill, the couple to whom I gave premarital counseling. I asked if my statement about marrying a stranger made sense to them, and they both said yes. Let's pick up the conversation where I left off.

"Once again let me go back to my question of a few minutes ago. Jan and Bill, what is it going to take, in addition to what we have already pointed out, for the two of you to understand each other and no longer be foreigners? What do you think, Bill? What do you feel, Jan?"

Bill thought a minute and then said, "Well, we need to speak the other person's language, right?"

"Right, but how do you do that, Bill? What does that mean in actual day-to-day communication?"

Mirror the Other Person's Language

Just then Jan spoke up, "I might be off on this, but I'm beginning to catch a sense of what you've been doing with us."

"What's that?" I asked.

"I've noticed," Jan continued, "that, yeah, now that I think about it, you really have been doing this. You talk differently to Bill and me. Now I know what you mean by speaking the other person's language. Bill, have you grasped it yet? No, let me take that back. Bill, do you see what Norm has been doing?"

With that switch in her vocabulary, I couldn't help but laugh. "You did it, Jan, you really do understand. You switched from your vocabulary, which made sense to you, and used a word that's part of Bill's vocabulary. Bill, did you notice that?"

"Well, I noticed something different, but I'm not sure yet."

"Go on, Jan," I encouraged her.

"Bill," she said, "you use words like *see, look, focus* all the time with me and everyone else, so they must have some significance to you. Those aren't my words, but I can learn to use them. When I use feeling words, I don't usually get much response from you, so perhaps I need to listen to your words more, and you need to listen to mine, and we can both learn to use each other's way of speaking."

Bill looked at Jan a minute and then slowly said, "Okay, I think I'm beginning to see—" He caught himself and then said, "You're right. I do use that word a lot." "You know," Jan continued, "if we had a tape recording of this session— no, if we had a tape recording and a video recording, like the ones we used in our teacher-education courses—I imagine we would discover that Norm has been doing more than using our language. Norm, is that right?"

"Yes, it is," I replied. "You're perceptive to sense that so soon."

Jan smiled and said, "Now, if you had made that same statement to Bill, how would you have said it?"

I laughed, "Bill, you're going to have to watch out for Jan. She really can see things quickly."

We all laughed at my choice of Bill's words, and Bill exclaimed loudly, "I do see it now. You might say the same thing to each of us, but with different words, based on how we talk. I just noticed something else, Norm. When you talk to me, you give a bit more volume to what you say. Yeah, you do. You raise your voice just a bit, because I talk louder than Jan does. I noticed something else, too. You don't waste any words with me on long explanations. You seem to make it short and to the point, and I like that. Maybe that's because that's the way I talk. This is really something. We haven't been here long, but it seems as if we've been together or known each other for a long time."

Jan broke in, "Yes, I agree. I feel, and that's one of my comfortable words, the same way. I've noticed Norm does more than just speak our language with his choice of words. When he talks to you, he seems to shift in his chair and sits almost the way you do. It's nothing major, but he has done this several times. He sits up a bit more, which is the way you sit, Bill. When you talk to me, Norm, I've noticed you tend to sit back and put your hands on the arm of the chair, which is exactly what I do. You even slow down your rate of speaking and speak more softly to me than to Bill."

"You're right, Jan," I replied, "and I feel good about what you are sharing for several reasons. One is, I want to be sensitive to the people I talk with, whether it is in this office or outside of the counseling environment. Second, I am not always consciously thinking of my choice of words or my body language. What you've just said lets me know that this way of responding to people is becoming more and more automatic for me. I'm delighted to see how quickly both of you are grasping this concept."

Consciously Communicate

"Since the two of you are just now becoming aware of this process," I continued, "it will take some work on your part to refine your communication with each other. I feel you've discovered the fact that you have probably responded this way already with other people, and you just were not aware of it. Now you will become more aware and will work consciously on how you communicate, not only with each other, but in a wider range of contacts as well. What will each of you be doing differently in your communication with each other at this point? Bill, what do you think?"

Bill responded, "Well, since this is in my lap, let me think a minute." He paused a while, considering my question. "Boy, this is something. I feel as if—how do you like that, one of Jan's favorite words!—I've just come back from an archeological expedition and made a gigantic discovery, and I'm still trying to put together all the pieces I've unearthed!"

At this point, I broke in, "Bill, is that the way you usually describe things? Jan, was that a typical description for Bill?" They looked at each other, wondering who was supposed to answer. I responded with both hands open, looking from one to the other, saying nonverbally, "Whoever wants to respond may do so."

Jan spoke, "I haven't heard descriptions like that too often, but it was great. It said so much more than, 'I'm thinking about it,' or something to that effect."

"Well," Bill said, "it's just the way I was feeling, and that's the best way to describe it."

"Bill, that was great," I said. "That was a beautiful example of how to expand your description and give your conversation more life, meaning, and richness. As you begin to communicate more and more like that, you will be amazed at your own ability and other people's response to you."

"Sometimes," Bill answered, "I even amaze myself! Well, here is what I'm going to be doing differently as I communicate with you, Jan. I guess the first step is to really learn your language, and that means I need to listen to you, to what you say, and how you say it. I'll have to listen to you with my eyes as well as my ears. I know that there are times when I don't have eye contact with you when you talk; then when I do turn and look at you, your message somehow seems different.

"I don't think I will totally change my way of communicating, since I want to be me. *But* when I talk with you, I can use some of your words and phrases. Would it help if I didn't talk as loudly or as fast?"

"Well," Jan replied, "I hadn't thought about it. Sometimes I do feel less on edge when you slow down and are a bit quieter. But I don't want you not to be yourself, so let's play it by ear and see how I feel."

"Okay," Bill continued. "I could do that, I know. I know something that might help. What about my giving more detail when I share with you? Maybe I can expand my two lines into four, when I tell you a story or event," Bill grinned as he said it.

"Bill, that's an excellent idea," I commented. "You do give more detail than some men I've worked with. I've seen some who seem to reflect the old John Wayne silent-cowboy image. They sit here and say, 'Yup,' and, 'Nope,' and that's it. It's like pulling teeth to get any more out of them. You know what I did with one fellow one day? He'd had so much pressure put on him to talk more, and it hadn't worked, so I decided to take a totally opposite approach. I suggested to him that he *not* share any more than he had been and that he continue to respond with his typical words or, 'Yup,' and, 'Nope.' When he asked me questions, I began to respond to him with his same words, and did he look surprised! Once he saw what it was like, he began to open up and communicate, and we all discovered that he could share details. Bill, give more detail, and Jan will respond more and will also put less pressure on you to share, since you're already doing it. At times *I* have just given summary statements. Most men have this tendency. Now when I hear of a friend or acquaintance who has had a baby, instead of going home and telling Joyce the fact, with none of the vital statistics, I write down the particulars, such as sex, name, weight, length, when born, and so on. Then I share that information, since that's what she wants to hear. I used to go home and say, 'So-and-so had a baby.' Joyce would ask, 'Oh, what was it? A boy or a girl? When? How much did it weigh?' I would answer, 'Oh, I don't know. It was a kid. That's all I know.' That doesn't go over too well at my house.

"Jan, when you share with Bill, condense a bit and give the topic and bottom line first, and you will have his attention."

There was no question that rapport had been established during that initial session. We related very well together. Why? Because I took the initiative and learned their language. I did not wait for them to learn mine or make them conform to mine at the outset. Notice that they were very open to take my suggestions for new ways to communicate. Why did that occur so readily? Because of my pacing, a subject you'll find out more about in the next chapter.

Who are you most like, Jan or Bill? What is your style of communication? What will be your first step as you begin to incorporate these principles into your life in a new way?

Remember:

Speak the other person's language.

Energy Builders

1. Have you ever known someone who had a communication style so different from yours that you found it hard to understand each other? What happened?

2. What does *rapport* mean? Do you have an easy time developing rapport with others? Do you develop it most quickly with those who are like you? Why? How can you increase your rapport with those who are different from you?

3. What does *mirroring* mean? How is it different from mimicking? How can you mirror someone else's nonverbal messages? Verbal communication?

4. How can you refine your communication with others? Do you speak the same language? What will be three benefits of speaking the other person's language? Give an example of how you did this today.

5. What will you do this week with the information in this chapter? Describe how your communication will be different.

Seven

What's Your Speed? Pacing and Rapport Building

In mirroring you reflect another person's nonverbal communication. *Pacing* is very similar, except that it also includes the verbal aspects of communication, using the same or similar terminology as the person to whom you are talking. You simply meet another person where he or she is or match them in some way. Pacing involves becoming like another person so you can establish rapport and gain the person's attention, friendship, and influence. It involves responding with similar language, body postures, gestures, voice tone, tempo, and so on. The more adept you become at this, the more comfortable you will feel in relating to a wider group of individuals. When you pace, you are saying, "I am like you in some ways, and you are safe with me. You can trust me." The more flexible you are, the more influence and persuasive power you will have with others. People locked into a rigid manner of responding, who demand that others accept them exactly as they are, limit their potential, experiences, and relationships.

Pace Yourself to Others' Moods

You may use pacing even with something as abstract as moods. Moods look for companionship of a similar kind, and difference in them has been the downfall of many a marriage. For example, how do you wake up in the morning? Is it a slow, laborious process in which one eye makes it open while you debate whether or not to open the other one? Does it take five minutes for the message from the brain to hit your leg muscles and tell them to move your leg over the edge of the bed, while the rest of your body tries to hide under the covers? Do you grope for the door and the hallway leading to the kitchen so you can inhale your caffeine fix that will get your body moving? Do you finally come alive an hour or two later?

If the above description fits you, chances are good you're married to the opposite type. This individual leaps from bed in the morning with his or her brain already in high gear ready to face the day. Such people come in several varieties. Ever heard of the commander? This guy awakens giving orders. If you're his spouse, you feel as though you should salute! The commander starts the day with, "Okay, we have ten minutes to get into the kitchen. I want French toast, bacon, and orange juice, freshly squeezed. Come on, come on, get up. You take your shower first, and I'll give you three minutes, then I'll shave, and then you. . . ." If you're the one in slow gear, you feel like shooting this guy!

Or there's the efficiency expert, "John, I tell you every morning, if you wake up at six-thirty instead of seven you'd have five minutes for your shave, six minutes for your shower, and eight minutes to dress. Then when you came to breakfast it would all be taken care of. Now on your way home, I'd like you to stop and—" Hearing something like this each morning would make me want to hide in the shower for the rest of the day!

For some individuals, these differences have to do with the metabolism, since we all have a need for different amounts of sleep.

Pacing on the Job

When slower-moving individuals hit the office, they have to make quite an adjustment to get their adrenaline flowing. Here is where timing is very important. I believe the wide-awake go-getter needs to take responsibility for doing the pacing. Why? Because it is easier to slow down than to rev up!

I happen to be one of those wide-awake, energetic individuals in the morning. One of my seminar coordinators, however, needs a couple of hours before she can build up a full head of steam. When she does, she really moves! At first I would start the day full of ideas to discuss with her, but things didn't go well. She didn't receive my ideas very well. Soon I learned to give her time to get settled in the morning. Then I would amble in and chat for a few minutes. After a while, in an offhand manner, I would mention one idea, and we would talk a bit about it; then I would interject another idea, and we would discuss that. Before long we were on the same wavelength.

It was easier for me to slow down and match her mood than for her to speed up. Soon we were able to work at the same pace.

If you have co-workers who have different energy levels from yours at different times than you do, learn to adapt to their moods. If you need some time to get going in the morning, explain that to your co-workers and let them know the best way to approach you. It may help.

Pacing verbal communication is the key to building rapport. I heard the story of a man who used pacing in his contacts over the phone to increase his sales. He owned an answering service, and since he was familiar with the concept of pacing, he began to match the rate of speed of people who called in for information. He needed to make his phone conversations count, since this was basically his only contact. If the inquirer spoke rather slowly, he spoke slowly; if he spoke quickly, so did the salesman. He was pleasantly surprised to discover a 30 percent increase in his subscription rate, just from pacing his telephone conversations.

As I've said before, pacing volume also helps. If you speak softly, you usually appreciate someone else who also speaks softly. If someone speaks loudly, you soon discover that he respects you more for speaking at his volume level.

Recently a friend of mine recommended a new book, *Social Style/Management Style*. When I read it, I discovered they used some of the basic concepts I have been talking about here, but applied them very specifically to the business world. Robert and Dorothy Bolton talked about becoming flexible and adapting to other people:

> Just as the primary factor in vocational success is one's ability to work well with people, the reverse is also true. The prime cause of failure in virtually all types of work is unsatisfactory relationships. For decades research aimed at discovering the primary reasons for the termination of employees has provided surprisingly consistent results—about 80 percent are fired because of poor interpersonal relationships.
>
> Of the people important to your success, 75 percent are very different from you. They use time differently, make decisions differently, prefer to relate in different ways, and have different styles of communicating. . . . To sum up, high interpersonal flexibility is now asso-

ciated with business success and probably will be an even more important factor in the coming years.[1]

A major concept of this outstanding book emphasizes Style Flex. This means a person temporarily adjusts his behavior to encourage others to act more productively with him. Style Flex assists you in communicating your ideas to others. You can move onto the other person's wavelength without losing your own integrity or your naturalness. The authors also define four types of social styles and give specific guidelines for becoming flexible and responding to others in their own style. This is another form of pacing and speaking another person's language. (The Boltons have pamphlets available for applying their concepts to marriage and parenting. Training workshops are also available, and I would recommend this book and their concepts to anyone.)[2]

Developing the flexibility to use words, phrases, and images familiar to other people is an important skill. When you do this, you tell the person you understand him and he can trust you.

When shouldn't you attempt to pace? There are obvious times such as talking with someone who has a tic, who stutters, or has an accent, behavior, or speech that is contrary to your belief or value system.

Learn How to Lead

Let's go back to Jan and Bill. Remember I asked you why they responded so readily to my suggestions? It was because I used pacing and spoke their language. But I also wanted to teach them this model so that once we had established rapport I could *lead* them to this new information. *Leading* means we do something different from what the person is doing.

Too often many of us make the mistake of attempting to lead without first establishing rapport. If I had started my session with Bill and Jan by telling them about the process without taking the time to establish rapport and letting them experience it, I could have saved my breath, because it would have fallen on deaf ears. Teachers, lecturers, and ministers often violate this principle. Unfortunately, some feel they deserve a hearing just because of who they are or what they do. Even when you work with a large group of individuals or teach a good-sized group, you can discover ways to establish rapport that will make people more receptive to your words.

Often I conduct seminars with anywhere from 50 to 400 people in attendance. Because I desire things to go smoothly and properly, usually everything has been checked two or three times, and all is in order before the first person walks in the door for the seminar. I also want to be free of last-minute details so I can greet the people, find out where they come from, and just have some personal interaction with them. When I stand up to teach, I have already established some rapport with many of them and can evaluate the responsiveness and personality of the group within the first few minutes.

To measure their level of responsiveness and create a greater degree of response, at the beginning of my presentation I often ask the group to turn around, find someone they haven't met yet, and introduce themselves. The volume level lets me know how responsive they may be as we begin the seminar.

Over the years I've also discovered the value of speaking positively. In our Marriage Renewal Seminar, there are several times when we have the couples meet in groups to discuss their responses to questions and several times when the couples sit face-to-face, holding hands and talking one-on-one. "You are going to have the opportunity," I say, "to do something many people really enjoy. You are going to have several minutes to sit face-to-face as a couple and respond to these questions." Again and again I emphasize the word *opportunity*. Later in the day I reinforce it by pointing out something most of them already know. I tell them, "I am helping you rediscover a model of communication that we often let slide the longer we are married: talking face-to-face.

In fact the longer we are married, the more we learn to communicate doing two or three things at the same time. We do dishes, yell from one room to the next, have the TV on, prepare dinner, and so on. We miss out on so much because of our lack of eye contact." I can tell from their looks and head gestures that I have struck a responsive chord.

Another method of establishing rapport in a classroom setting occurs in my graduate class at the seminary where I have taught for the past twenty years. For the first few weeks I begin each class by asking the students to pair up by twos and take a minute to construct a personal question they would like to ask me about my life. At first the students are quite hesitant and wonder if I mean what I say. They wonder about the limitations to the questions. During the first couple of class sessions, the questions reflect their hesitation and are somewhat general and safe. But in time they realize they can ask me whatever they like, and the hands spring up and questions become increasingly personal. They become more open, and I become more open, and we establish rapport more quickly and at a deeper level than it would have had this not occurred.

Build your relationships first, and the other person will be willing to consider what you have to say and what you would like him or her to do![3]

How can you build your relationships? Pace—with your moods, language, posture, tone, and volume. Be flexible!

Energy Builders

1. What does *pacing* mean? What message does it give to another person? Are you flexible enough to use it in your communication?

2. What does it mean to pace yourself to another person's moods? Have you done this with someone at work? At home?

Have you successfully used other kinds of pacing at work? At home? Give two examples for each of these questions.

3. Can you have people respond readily to your suggestions if you do not develop rapport with them first? Why or why not? Is this true of large groups, too?

4. What will you do this week with the information in this chapter? Describe how your communication will be different.

Eight

Do You See What I See, Hear What I Hear, And Feel What I Feel?

Three men stood talking to each other. One said to his two friends, "Anyone knows that seeing is believing."

The man next to him turned and said, "Oh, no, Fred, hearing is believing."

"I hate to inform you," the third man countered, "but you're both wrong. Feeling is believing."

Who is right? Who is wrong in this discussion? They all

are. For some people seeing is believing, for others hearing is believing, and for a third group feeling or sensing is believing.

How Do You Perceive Things?

How do you respond to life? Do you *see* things more? Do you *hear* things more? Do you sense or *feel* things more? We all respond to what is occurring around us through one of these three ways. Our perception of the world around us is created through our visual, auditory, kinesthetic (or feeling), and our olfactory/gustatory (smell and taste) senses. Because of the influences upon us and our experiences with our environment, we tend to develop or lean upon one of these senses or intake systems more than the others. We use them all, but we rely more heavily upon one of them.

You may be an auditorally oriented person. You tend to depend upon spoken words for your information. If you are visually oriented, you use your eyes to perceive your world around you, and you use visual images in remembering and thinking. If you're a kinesthetically oriented individual, you tend to feel your way through your experiences. Both internal and external stimuli are sorted through your feelings and these feelings determine your decisions. In our culture, very few people rely just upon smell and taste.

An individual in a scientific profession would have an easier time of it if his or her dominant mode of perception were visual rather than kinesthetic. Having feelings about scientific formulas or equations is not really going to prove very helpful. On the other hand, someone studying ballet would find it easier if he or she had a highly developed kinesthetic sense.

When I was in junior high school, I remember the band and orchestra members took tests each year. We listened to various tones and pitches to determine our ability. Some students made some very fine auditory distinctions; these individuals had an auditory bent or inclination. The intake system we use will affect the way we respond to and cope with life.

Even though we have one dominant sense, we may increase our use of our other senses. For a number of reasons I've learned to do this over the years. My primary sensing apparatus has been visual. I'm not sure why, except that I know it was highly emphasized and reinforced when I was a child. I read extensively, and perhaps that helped create the imaginative pictures in my mind. I also learned to sight-read music very well between the ages of six and twelve. At times I am still frustrated by those individuals who cannot read a note of music, but if you hum a tune for them, they can play fifteen variations on that theme. My orientation is visual. Theirs is auditory.

My visual side frequently comes to the forefront. If one of my secretaries comes into my office and says, "Norm, here's an interesting letter. Let me read it to you." Without thinking I will respond with, "Oh, let me see it." I like to read things because I process them faster that way. Invariably I ask people to "send it to me in writing," or, "put your suggestions down in writing and turn them in to me so I can see them." Recently I heard the story of several office employees who felt frustrated about getting their requests and ideas across to a vice-president. They approached the man and talked with him, and at times he appeared interested, but nothing ever came of their time spent with him. When three of these employees discussed the problem with their office manager, he made a simple suggestion: "It isn't as though your ideas are not good. They just are not registering with him. I think he is a person who, like it or not, needs everything to come to his attention in writing. I know this means a little extra work for you, but let's try presenting everything in writing. This doesn't mean that you can't share your ideas in person, but at the same time have it typed out in detail, and let's see what happens." They grumbled a bit, but followed the suggestion. Were they surprised when their ideas, which their boss had apparently discarded before, were now accepted! Why? Because the vice-president was a visual person and liked to have his information in writing. When his employees began to talk his language, he began to listen!

When I hear new ideas or concepts, whether they are simple or complex, my visual side begins to think, *How can I diagram these concepts and put them on an overhead transparency so I can convey them better to those I teach?*

Let's summarize what I have been *saying* to *see* if you're in *touch* with it yet. (Notice I used words for all three senses.) We have three main senses—hearing, seeing, and feeling. We prefer one over the other two for perceiving life, storing our experiences, and making decisions. How do we discover which sense we prefer? Our *language* gives it away.

The visual person uses terms like:

> I *see* what you're saying.
> That *looks* good to me.
> I'm not too *clear* on this right now.
> This is still a bit *hazy* to me.
> Boy, when they asked that question, I just went *blank*.
> That sheds a new *light* on the problem.
> Do you pick up my *perspective?*

Here are some of the most typical words you will hear coming from the visual person:

focus	colorful
see	pretty
clear	peek
bright	glimpse
picture	imagine
perspective	notice
show	color
hazy	

The auditory person uses terms like:

> That *rings* a bell with me.
> It *sounds* real good to me.

I *hear* you.
I'm trying to *tune* in to what you're saying.
Listen to this new idea.
I had to *ask* myself.
Now, that idea *clicks* with me.

Here are some of the most typical words you will hear coming from an auditory person:

listen	loud
yell	shout
talk	told
hear	tone
harmony	sounds
noisy	say
discuss	amplify
call	

The kinesthetic person will use phrases such as these:

I can't get a *handle* on this.
I've got a good *feeling* about this project.
Can you get in *touch* with what I'm saying?
It's easy to *flow* with what they're saying.
I don't *grasp* what you're trying to do.
This is a *heavy* situation.

Some of the typical words used are:

feel	irritated
firm	clumsy
touch	pushy
pressure	relaxed
tense	grab
concrete	soft
hurt	handle
touchy	smooth

Some words we commonly use have no relationship to any of these three senses. They are:

know	need
think	experience
remember	decide
change	negotiate
want	pretend

What is your strongest sense? Are you aware of it? Had you considered this idea before? I find it easy to close my eyes and picture in my mind an experience from the past or an anticipated experience. When I read a novel, I see the action in my mind, in vivid color, and could describe all the visual details. But this would be difficult for other people. I might find it hard to experience the smell of a flower in my mind. I could work at it, but for others it would be easier. Some people can hear the sound of life all around them just by thinking. Some individuals have very vivid mental images, where others have faded images and some none at all. Some of us see sentences in our mind.

As you talk with others, you may wonder which is their dominant sense. How can you discover this? There are times when it really isn't apparent, and you won't know at first which form of communication will work best. So you need to experiment. If you are not sure which sensing mode is dominant, vary your questions. Ask, "Does this idea *look* all right to you?" "How do you *feel* about investing in this new program?" If one approach does not seem to work after a while, switch to another, and if that doesn't work, try the third.

What we sometimes perceive as resistance on the part of other people may not be resistance at all. We're just speaking the wrong language, and we need to change. Sometimes it helps to ask people how they would like the information presented. They will appreciate your sensitivity and your willingness to learn their language.

I remember a man who approached me one time and said, "Norm, I would like to go over this new program with you, and I can do it in two ways. I can let you see it first and read over the summary pages and then ask me questions, or I can sit down with you and explain it to you step by step. Which would you prefer?" Which one do you think I chose? You're right. I read and then asked questions.

A sales representative approached me one day and said, "Norm, I have this new testing program you've just got to hear about. I have been looking forward to telling you all about it, so you can really get a feel for what we're going to be doing." I wasn't as positive about this person's approach. But someone else from the same company called later and said, "Norm, I've been wondering if you would be interested in learning about our new program. You might want to see where we're going. I can do two things. I can give you a brief summary over the phone, and then you can let me know how it looks to you, and we can proceed in more detail. Or I can stop by with an overview and go through the entire program step by step. Which would you prefer?" He spoke my language by using my terminology and giving me a choice.

Pacing and Perception

Let's go back to our word from the previous chapter: *pacing*. The most effective way of applying this new information is to incorporate it into pacing. Pacing is what I did with Bill and Jan. In that situation I was able to be flexible enough to incorporate their vocabulary into my own. It takes more work when you are talking with two different individuals and they speak two different languages, but it's worth the effort.

Let's look now at some conversations and label the people by the words *visual, kinesthetic* and *auditory*.

> *Visual:* "Honey, if you would look over that new room arrangement again, you will see that I've taken your needs into consideration. I have focused on the important places in the room. It looks good to me. I don't see what you're so bothered about."
> *Kinesthetic:* "I don't know. . . . I just keep getting the feeling that something about it is wrong. I've just got this sense about it. You know, I can't put my finger on it. . . . It's just a bit uncomfortable."

Visual: "Oh, come on. You're just stuck in your own point of view about this. Look at it from my perspective. The room is brighter this way, and we have more walking space. Stand over here and look around the room."

Kinesthetic: "I don't know. I don't think you're in touch with how I feel about this room. I just can't get a handle on it, but if we leave it this way, it just isn't going to work."

What is happening in this conversation? Well, we do have two points of view (there's my visual coming out again!). But the main problem is that they're talking right past each other. They are not connecting. One uses words referring to how he sees things, and the other's words reflect how she feels. Let's listen in on another discussion between a visual and an auditory.

Auditory: "John, I want to talk with you about something that we've spoken about before. I know we're ready to move on the room addition, but I've still got some ideas, and I want to know how these sound to you. Now, please hear me out, because they are a bit involved."

Visual: "Well, do you have them outlined for me? Let me see them first, and then we can act on them. That will save a lot of time as well, since I've got a lot going on right now."

Auditory: "Well, they're not that finalized yet. I've just started to tune into them, and I thought we could discuss them. You know, I do want to have some say in the final outcome."

Visual: "Oh, I agree. You need to have your views reflected in this new addition. But for me to focus in on what you're trying to present, I would like you to have something definite to show me. Why don't you formulate it clearly, and then let's talk."

Again miscommunication. They are talking two different languages, but if one or both could change, they would connect.

Here is an example of pacing with all three approaches. It can be done!

> *Visual:* "As I look over these plans for the new room arrangement you showed me, I have some more questions about it. I'm just not clear where we are going to put all of the old and new furniture."
>
> PACE: "Well, I think I can see where your concern is coming from. Maybe it's not all that clear to me either, but let me try to paint a picture of what's inside my head. I guess I need to illustrate this for both of us so we can discover the solution."
>
> *Auditory:* "John, let's talk some more about the new addition. I listened to your thoughts last night, and since I've had some time to consider them, I wonder if we're really on the same wavelength. Now, here's what I want to say."
>
> PACE: "All right, I hear you. I'll try to tune into your thoughts on this room. I want it to be comfortable for both of us. I sure want us to be in harmony over this room, since we have to live with it for the next few years."
>
> *Kinesthetic:* "I'm sorry, but I just can't seem to get in touch with what you're saying. It just isn't concrete enough for me to grab on to it. I want this room to feel comfortable to me and everyone else. So far what you've been describing to me just doesn't seem to fit."
>
> PACE: "Well, I understand what you're feeling. We are connecting on this, even though it doesn't feel that way for you."

The person pacing was able to fit his or her vocabulary to the other person's. This is a classic example of speaking the other person's language. In fact, this was an example of translation. The pacer translated his language to fit that of the other person. You can act as a translator when you talk with other people.

You can also act as a translator for two people who tend to speak different languages. Let's go back to Jan and Bill again. Bill said, "She keeps showing me her ideas for the wedding dinner, but it doesn't make sense to me. She wants it to look right, but the way it's set up now it appears to be unorganized, and there's not enough time allotted between the different events. But she can't seem to see this."

Jan chimed in at this point and said, "Bill, you're just insensitive to what's important to my family. Mom and Dad and I talked, and we feel this is the best way to have the dinner. You just can't get in touch with the fact that others do things differently, and it can work. After all, Dad is footing the bill for this part of it, too, so they have a right to be involved."

I jumped in at this point, since they were not hearing each other, and said, "Bill, I think that Jan is just trying to show you that even though you have a different perspective, it will work out. She would like you to see it from her family's point of view. Jan, perhaps you could try to sense where Bill is coming from. Perhaps he feels a bit overwhelmed because your family is pulling together. Why not clear it up for him; then you would end up feeling more comfortable about it." They both seemed to hear me when I presented the solution in that manner. Their language and thinking is different. The language of feelings is different from the language of sight, and the language of sound is different from the other two.

Let's consider this approach in the field of business. Here is an example concerning the presentation of a house to prospective buyers. As you read the three descriptions below, which house appeals to you the most?

The following material reprinted by permission of the author and Publisher, Robert Dilts—APPLICATIONS OF NEURO-LINGUISTIC PROGRAMMING 1983 META PUBLICATIONS, CUPERTINO, CA USA

1. This house is quite picturesque, with a quaint look about it. You can see that a lot of focus has been put on the colorful patio and garden area. The house has a lot of window space so that you can enjoy the view. It is clearly a good buy.

2. This house is soundly constructed and well situated. It is in such a quiet area that all you hear when you walk outside are the sounds of the birds singing. Its storybook interior has so much character you'll probably be asking yourself how you could ever pass it by.

3. This house is not only solidly constructed, it has a special feel to it. It's not often that you come in contact with a place that touches on so many important features. It is spacious enough that you really feel you can move around freely, yet cozy enough that you won't wear yourself out taking care of it.

Which home did you choose?

Perhaps you have figured it out—all three descriptions fit the same house. Each was written to appeal to a different sense. If you leaned toward the first house, you are probably more visually (sight) oriented. If you were more impressed with the second house, you are probably auditorally (sound) oriented. And if you preferred the third, you are most likely feeling oriented.[1]

You may think of other business areas where you will be able to apply this type of communication process

Sense Appeal

Whether or not we realize it, we encounter numerous examples of appealing to the three sense areas every day. Ad writers take these ideas into consideration; authors endeavor to paint word pictures that appeal to all three senses. So do teachers.

Often, when I teach, I will ask my students to close their eyes and use their imaginations as I share an experience with them. One such example is from the beginning of our Marriage Renewal Seminar:

Before beginning any journey, you must select a path. One path out of many possible paths. And you don't always know the terrain you will cover until you start.

Unlike the average high-country hiker, a person starting out on the marriage path can't pore over a forest-service map or interrogate a ranger about the trail ahead. Neither does he have the advantage of trailside signs telling him in advance the exact distance or whether the trail is classified as easy, moderate or difficult.

Picture a hiker standing at the base of a mountain. He must select a path. Not one of the paths is completely level; not one of them is an easy downhill glide. Each of them would involve work, energy, patience, endurance, and a steady pace.

As he steps onto a trail and begins the gradual ascent, the hiker has the time to note and delight in his surroundings. He is fresh and rested. He sets a moderate pace. Having made adequate physical preparation, he does not feel winded or weary. He takes in the sounds of the wildlife and the wind in the trees. His sense of smell awakens to the aroma of forest and flower. His eyes cradle scenes of vivid paintbrush and columbine, aspen bark and budding pine cone, the stationary chipmunks on rocks and stumps, and the ever-alert hawk gliding silently overhead. By stopping occasionally the hiker is able to fully enjoy and feel the delight of all of his senses coming alive.

Another fun activity that we conduct later in the seminar is a facetious compatibility test based upon how they peel an orange. I tell the group: "I would like you to close your eyes and, using the gift of imagination that God has given you, visualize yourself seated at a table. On the table is a bowl of big, ripe, juicy oranges. See yourself reaching out to the bowl and as you select an orange, you feel the texture of the skin. As you begin to peel off the skin, the juice begins to run out, and you smell the aroma of the ripe orange. You begin to anticipate sinking your teeth into the soft pulp and experiencing the sweetness of the fruit."

Some people even begin to salivate just by thinking about the experience!

As you listen to movies, television, teachers, or ministers, notice (there's a visual word again!) how the information is being presented to you. Some ads, lectures, sermons, or illustrations that do not appeal to you would appeal if the person giving the presentation put it into your language. If people are not responding to us, perhaps it's because we are not putting our responses into their language!

Some writers have an uncanny ability with words. Dr. Charles Swindoll is one of my favorite authors. I like what he says, but he also appeals to me because he gives such detail that I can construct pictures in my head. Here is one example:

> Blow that layer of dust off the book of Nahum in your Bible and catch glimpse of the last part of verse 3, chapter 1. "The way of the Lord is in the whirlwind and in the storm . . . " (MLB).
>
> That's good to remember when you're in a rip-snortin', Texas frog-strangler as I was a few weeks back. I nudged myself to remember God's presence as the rain-heavy, charcoal clouds hemorrhaged in eerie, aerial explosions of saw-toothed lightning and reverberating thunder. Witnessing that atmospheric drama, I reminded myself of its Director who was, once again, having His way in the whirlwind and the storm.[2]

A different emphasis is expressed in this brief excerpt from the same book:

> *Children.* They express their feelings. Deep down in their fragile, inner wells are a multitude of needs, questions, hurts, and longings. Like a tiny bucket, their tongues splash out these things. The busy, insensitive, preoccupied parent, steamrolling through the day, misses many a cue and sails right past choice moments never to be repeated.[3]

What a sharp ability to visualize Dr. Swindoll shows in his descriptive writing. You have no doubt that he *sees* things—he's a visual sort of person.

Psychologists may also use the appeal to the senses to help people who do not have a clear, positive image of themselves. In counseling, a psychologist may help a client overcome worry or negative thinking by helping him replace his negative pictures of himself with positive images. Here is an example of how a person can eliminate worry about preparing for a presentation by using visual role rehearsal:

Sit or lie down. Make yourself comfortable. Close your eyes. Breathe in and out slowly and deeply. Allow yourself to relax. Deepen this relaxation by whichever technique works best for you. Go to a level where you can visualize, where images flow freely and easily. Allow an image to come to mind of a meeting room where you have been asked to give a talk. Picture yourself in the front of the room. Look across the room. Notice details—the color of walls, where the door is and what it's made of. Notice the windows and pictures on the walls. Now look at the chairs; notice how they are arranged and what they are made of. Look at the people. Notice the kinds of clothes they are wearing. See if you recognize any friends or colleagues in the group. Now imagine walking over to a table or lectern to begin your talk. Notice what the table is made of, put your hands on it and feel it. Take a few deep breaths until you feel calm, clear and relaxed. Listen as the people in the audience quiet down. Allow the quietness to enter you and make you calm. See the people looking at you in a friendly, interested way. Now hear yourself begin the lecture. Your voice is clear and loud enough for everyone to hear. Your speech is organized, interesting, and conveys exactly what you wish to say. As you're speaking, you feel increasingly confident and comfortable. You can tell from the looks on their faces that the people in the audience have understood what you've said and are stimulated by it. As you end the lecture you hear excited talk begin among members of the audience. A number of people come up to you with stimulating questions and you answer them readily.[4]

Appeal to Senses and Avoid Resistance

Do other individuals respond to your requests, or do you frequently experience frustration because they don't? Are you sometimes confused as to why a perfectly logical request or approach on your part meets with resistance? If so, perhaps you have presented the request in such a way that it doesn't make sense to the person, or it doesn't capture his attention because you have not used his language.

Maybe you've had it happen in something as simple as making a suggestion to your spouse about what you would like to do for a vacation. If you neglect to present it according to what your spouse would enjoy doing, you might get turned down.

John had a great idea for a vacation (or so it seemed to him), but when he presented it to his wife, Joan, she appeared uninterested and negative. As he told me in a counseling session, "I can't understand her. You've suggested that we take some time together and rebuild our relationship, but when I sprang this great idea on her for a trip to Mexico, she threw cold water on it."

I replied, "John, you said you sprang this idea on her. Tell me exactly how you approached her."

"Well," he said, "when I got home, I just came in the front door and yelled to her, 'Honey, I've got this great plan for a ten-day vacation for us, and we can go next month. Where are you? I want to show this to you.' And then I found her in the kitchen, getting dinner ready, and I said, 'Look at this. A ten-day vacation in Mexico at a price we can afford. Take a look at this brochure. I've checked my schedule at the office, and in five weeks I'm clear, and we can leave. Look at these pictures of the sandy beach, and the fishing there is great! They take you out in these little boats, so you don't have to fight the crowds, and you're away from the busy cities. Just think—ten days to bum around the beach, barefoot, cooking fresh fish over the coals. Isn't that great?' But she didn't seem interested."

"Does Joan enjoy having you spring a surprise on her, or does she enjoy being a part of the process of selecting something?" I asked.

John thought a minute, "Hmm . . . , no, I guess she likes to be involved in looking things over and giving her input."

"All right, can she handle a lot of information all at one time, or does she prefer to have it presented a piece at a time so she can consider it, ask questions, and think about it?"

John sat silently for a minute, then said, "Wow! You're right. I guess I came on like a steamroller. She likes to think about things and take them a step at a time."

I continued, "You seemed to emphasize the things *you* enjoy doing. Are fishing, walking on a sandy beach, and cooking fresh fish her favorite activities on a vacation?"

John slumped in his chair, shook his head, and smiled, "Oh my. I can see what I did. You've been telling me to approach her in a way that makes her feel comfortable, and I did the wrong thing again. Of course fishing isn't her favorite activity on a vacation. She likes to fish a couple of hours a day for two or three days, but she enjoys sight-seeing and exploring new areas and shopping in new stores and visiting art galleries more. Man, if I had it to do all over again, I think I would have approached her with a few questions, to get her attention."

"John, what would some of those have been?"

He thought a moment and told me, "All right, if I were to do it over again, I would have gone home, and after we had talked about the day, I would have asked, 'Have you ever dreamed of sleeping in in the morning and then lounging under the palm trees while you eat breakfast?' If she asked why, I could have said, 'Oh, no real reason. I just thought I'd ask.' Later I would say, 'Have you ever thought of exploring Mayan ruins with your camera to see what you could discover? How would that feel to you?' If I did that, after a while, she would stop everything and say, 'All right, something is up. You're not just asking questions to be asking. There's a reason, and I am curious. What are you getting at?' Then she would *want* to know. You're right. We *are* different. I approached her the way *I* would want to be approached. But I ran over her. I think I can save the day though. I'm going to develop a new plan, and I think she'll hear me this time." His wife did hear him because of a different presentation.

How do you express your ideas to your family members and associates or committee members? In your language or theirs? Even varying the kinds of questions we use helps the other individual realize that we can relate to his world and his way of responding to life.

Visual questions and statements:

> It appears to you. . . .
> You see it in this way. . . .
> Do you see it that way?
> How does it appear to you?

Kinesthetic questions and statements:

> You are sort of feeling that. . . .
> You are communicating a sense of. . . .
> I somehow sense that you feel. . . .
> Are you saying that this makes you feel . . . ?

Auditory questions and statements:

> Listening to you, it seems as if. . . .
> I really hear you saying. . . .
> What would you like to express to her?
> I kind of hear you saying that. . . .

Keep an Eye on Eye Movements

Now let's consider the most unusual concept in this entire discussion. Have you ever talked to someone and noticed the person's eyes stray from looking at you directly? Perhaps the person glanced up and to the right for a moment or looked down and to the right. Have you been in a classroom setting either as a participant or as a teacher and noticed one of the class members gazing upward and to the left? Have you ever noticed the eye movements of two individuals as they carry on a conversation?

The eye movements of a child or an adult are not random movements. They have a specific purpose. Perhaps you wonder if by his lack of eye contact the person might be indicating that he is uncomfortable, simply not listening, or daydreaming. But there are other possibilities. Watching people's eyes as you converse with them, or even when you speak in front of a group, gives you a clue as to what they are thinking about. Does that sound like mind reading? Before you dismiss this idea read on. Listening with our eyes is an undeveloped skill for most of us, but this information will make you a better listener.

Eye movements are a doorway to a person's thoughts. For example, if a person shifts his up and to the right, he is in the process of *constructing a visual image.*

If a person shifts her eyes up and to the left, she is *recalling some previous images.*

Artwork and accompanying text on this page and the next reprinted by permission of the author and publisher, Robert Dilts—Applications of Neuro-Linguistic Programming 1983 Meta Publications, Cupertino, CA USA

If an individual keeps his eyes level and to the right, he is in the process of *constructing sounds.*

If the person keeps her eyes level and shifts them to the left, she is *remembering previously heard sounds.*

If the individual looks down and to the right, he is *experiencing feelings.*

If the person is looking down and to the left, she is probably *talking to herself.*

(Many left-handed individuals will be reversed right to left with respect to this chart.)[5]

If the study of eye movements seems like a radical idea, here is an example of the various eye movements and their meaning from my counseling experience with a man I'll call Frank. In a discussion with him I noticed the following: Frank looked up and to the left when he was *remembering* the *look* on his wife's face when he gave her a gift. As he talked about what he thought would happen as a result of taking his wife on a surprise trip, he looked up and to the right as he *constructed an image* of how she would respond. Later on in our discussion he looked down and to the left as he *talked to himself* about either of the previous pictures. As he *recalled a time* when his wife *shared* with him how much she loved him, he looked straight and level, but to the left. As he *constructed different ways* of sharing with his wife how much she means to him, he looked straight and level and to the right. As he *experienced the feeling* of being loved, he looked down and to the right.

What does all this mean? It means the more observant you are, the more sensitive you will become and the better you can communicate.

Let's consider this approach in the field of business. A customer and a real-estate agent have been talking for some time. The customer moves her eyes level and to the left and says, "I just keep getting the feeling that something is missing from this. But I can't put my finger on it." Look back at the suggestions concerning eye movement. Is the customer constructing new pictures, feeling something, talking to herself, or remembering images and pictures? No, she is probably remembering hearing something. The agent who is sensitive to this responds by saying, "Well, I'm glad you told me that. Is there something we will need to *talk* about? Are you still concerned about the *noise* problem in this neighborhood?"

In our conversations with people, the proper use of questions can encourage them to share what they are experiencing as well as convey to them our sensitivity to their feelings and circumstances. Too often we use general questions such as, "What are you thinking?" or, "What are you feeling?"

which may miss the mark. If the person you are talking to shifts his eyes up and to the right, how would you respond? You might say, "I wonder what picture is coming to your mind at this time?" or, "I wonder what it looks like to you?"

If the person looks up and to the left you could say, "I wonder what picture from your photo album is coming to your mind at this time?" If the person looks to the right but her eyes are level, you could say, "Perhaps you're beginning to hear how this sounds."

If the person is looking level and to the left, a question like, "How did that sound to you when you first heard it expressed?" would be appropriate. Or, "Do you remember hearing her make that statement to you?"

As the individual looks down and to the right you might respond with, "It appears you might be feeling something at this time," or, "I would like to catch the feeling you're experiencing at this time," or, "You appear to be sensing something at this moment."

As the person looks down and to the left you could respond, "If I could listen into your mind right now, I would wonder what you're saying."

Try experimenting with these ideas sometime. You might be surprised at the outcome. Ask a group of individuals the following questions and note their eye movements:

> I would like you to create an image in your mind of the type of dream house you would like to have.
> Remember back to the first car you ever owned or drove. What did it look like?
> I would like you to remember some of the first compliments your parents or your spouse ever gave you. What were they?

You will probably discover many individuals reflecting these eye movements. Notice that I said *many,* because not everyone will follow the suggested pattern. Some people are not that expressive.

Perhaps the information in this chapter is shockingly new,

and you have a difficult time accepting it. Before you make your final decision, however, give the ideas a try. As you are willing to change your style of communication and become more flexible, your communication with others may be revolutionized!

Remember the following:

Pace the individual by using his or her language and dominant sense. As you talk with others, you will become more aware of your own eye movements. You are now going to be sensitive to your eyes and what is occurring inside you. Believe me! It will happen. It has happened to me, and as a result I know myself much better.

"The hearing ear and the seeing eye, The Lord has made both of them" (Proverbs 20:12).

Energy Builders

1. What are the three forms of perception that are most common in our society? How can you tell which is the most important one in a person's life?

2. Which method of perception is your dominant one? How can you tell?

3. How can you use pacing and perception to better your communication? How can you act as translator for two people with different methods of perception?

4. How do people use sense appeal on a daily basis? How can you use your awareness of it to present your ideas effectively to others?

5. Have you watched another person's eye movements to find out what he's thinking about? Try noticing the ones outlined in this chapter and putting them into use in your communication.

6. What will you do this week with the information in this chapter. Describe how your communication will be different.

Nine

The Language of Feelings _____

James sat in my office, looking a bit dismayed and sounding even more so as he slumped in the wingback chair. He looked up at me and, with hands open in a frustrated gesture, said, "I just don't know what to say. I realize that I'm not great at communication, but this bit about sharing my feelings puzzles me. Half the time I don't even know what I'm feeling, let alone know how to describe it. What am I? Some kind of freak?"

"You sound both frustrated and confused," I responded. "But let me assure you, you are not alone in your predicament. Many, many men today are in your position. We're told that we need to share our feelings, and it would be healthier for us to do so, but it's like telling a crippled person to stand up and walk. It's more as if we're expressively handicapped, rather than emotionally dead. How can we share something we've never been taught? Who is going to help us?"

"That's it," James said. "I feel emotionally crippled. My father never shared his emotions or feelings much, so early in life I guess I got the message that for a man to have feelings or emotions meant he was weak. So those I did experience I just stuffed away, hoping they would disappear. But other people around me aren't letting me get away with that anymore. What can I do now?"

James had just asked an important question that I hear often in my practice.

What's in an Emotion?

Of the three areas of senses that we have been discussing—visual, auditory, and kinesthetic (or feeling)—the last is the most difficult for many, especially men. True, some women have difficulty as well, but in the North American culture it is predominately the man who suffers with this crippling "disease," as counseling and seminars over the past two decades have thoroughly documented. Women are more familiar with the language of emotion than men, because they have been encouraged and taught to express and value emotion. They have developed a language of emotions and feel comfortable with them.

Defining Emotions

In order to develop a language of emotions, we need to understand what they are and learn to become flexible in using them to communicate with others.

Technically we may define an *emotion* as "an acute disturbance or upset of the individual, which is revealed in behavior or conscious experience." Others have defined it more simply as "a sentiment."

How do emotions influence us? We often experience them as transitory responses to occurrences in our environment. They may be intense or slight and may arise from external or internal stimulation—a condition of the body or a thought in the mind. When we experience an emotion, not only do our behavior and thinking change, we also have widespread changes take place in the functioning of the viscera (smooth muscles, glands, heart, and lungs), which are initiated by factors within a psychological situation. In short, the whole being may react to emotions.

Usually we describe what goes on by saying, "I have a feeling . . . ," if, for instance, we remember something from the past. We may not use the word *emotion* at all, and we don't look at it in technical terms. Instead we are aware of its results in our lives. I've always liked what C. B. Eavey says about emotions in *Principles of Mental Health for Christian Living*:

> Nothing in us so defiles and destroys the beauty and the glory of living as do emotions; nothing so elevates, purifies, enriches, and strengthens life as does emotion. Through our emotions we can have the worst or the best, we can descend to the lowest depths, or we can rise to the highest heights. Every normal human being has a longing for the overflowing of natural emotion. Without capacity to experience emotions suitable to the situations we meet we would not be normal. Emotions of the right kind, expressed in the proper way, make life beautiful, full and rich, rob it of monotony, and contribute much to both the enjoyment and the effectiveness of living.

No doubt about it, emotions have a great impact on us, but it's up to us to use and develop them properly. Since He created us as emotional beings, our feelings are a gift to us from God. He has not intended that we squelch them or avoid them; instead He encourages us to use them wisely.

Look at the expression of emotions found in the Scriptures:

As grieved and mourning, yet [we are] always rejoicing; as poor [ourselves, yet] bestowing riches on many: as having nothing, and [yet in reality] possessing all things.

2 Corinthians 6:10 AMP

For God did not give us a spirit of timidity—of cowardice, of craven and cringing and fawning fear—but [He has given us a spirit] of power and of love and of calm and well-balanced mind and discipline and self-control.

2 Timothy 1:7 AMP

When angry, do not sin; do not ever let your wrath—your exasperation, your fury or indignation—last until the sun goes down.

Ephesians 4:26 AMP

I heard, and my [whole inner self] trembled, my lips quivered at the sound. Rottenness enters into my bones and under me—down to my feet—I tremble. I will wait quietly for the day of trouble and distress, when there shall come up against [my] people him who is about to invade and oppress them.

Habakkuk 3:16 AMP

And Abel brought of the first-born of his flock and of the fat portions. And the Lord had respect and regard for Abel and for his offering. But for Cain and his offering He had no respect or regard. So Cain was exceedingly angry and indignant, and he looked sad and depressed.

Genesis 4:4, 5 AMP

And Jacob served seven years for Rachel; and they seemed to him but a few days, because of the love he had for her.

Genesis 29:20 AMP

[Share others' joy], rejoicing with those who rejoice; and [share others' grief], weeping with those who weep.

Romans 12:15 AMP

Ed and Carol Neuenschwander give a beautiful description of emotion in their book *Two Friends in Love:*

> Our emotions are the movements of our soul. They are the sensations we experience that bear the labels of joy, grief, pain, disillusionment, love, delight, warmth, astonishment, fright. They are the stirrings of our inner persons reflected in our cellular shells. Also, emotions are the subterranean shifts in feeling we encounter that aren't necessarily activated by sight, hearing, taste, or smell—though they may be. These inside movements, stirrings, or sensations may change several times an hour. They may occur in multiples, forming duets and trios that sometimes produce harmony and at other times create dissonance.
>
> My reason for defining emotions is that those who have become emotionally sheltered have usually lost touch with the distinctions between thinking and feeling. So I believe those distinctions are worth restatement.
>
> Emotional expressions get beyond the talk about issues and events and people by themselves—they get down to talking about the inside influence those things have upon us, how we feel our lives are touched by them. Also, emotions differ from intellectual activity, which is basically characterized by deliberation, analysis, evaluation, and reflection. Perhaps I can best put it in perspective this way: *Emotional expression is thinking aloud from the heart instead of the head.*[1]

Barriers to Emotions

Why don't things always run smoothly with our emotions? Because both men and women sometimes create walls and barriers against their own feelings and in turn against involvement with others who tend to express their feelings. The language difference is too uncomfortable. We wall ourselves in and others out and become self-contained hermits or prisoners, even in the presence of other people.

Feelings make up one-third of our potential awareness. Our intellect and our will (or determination) make up the other two-thirds. Some people choose to live their lives functioning on two cylinders rather than on all three, which puts a strain on the vehicle. The other two cannot make up for our emotional silence and insensitivity. Feelings are guideposts as we travel through life. We send and receive signals for support, love, nurturance, and protection—all our basic needs. Feelings are there to inform us, not to threaten us.

Dr. Ken Druck has suggested some the ways in which men especially tend to appear emotionally unaffected and in control.

- Men rationalize a course of inaction by telling themselves, *What good is it going to do to talk about it? That's not going to change anything!*
- Men worry and worry internally, but never face what they really feel.
- Men escape into new roles or hide behind old ones.
- Men take the attitude that the "feelings" will pass and shrug them off as unimportant.
- Men keep busy, especially with work.
- Men change one feeling into another—becoming angry instead of experiencing hurt or fear.
- Men deny the feeling outright.
- Men put feelings on hold—put them in the file drawer and tend to forget what they were classified under.
- Feelings are confronted with drugs and alcohol.
- Men are excellent surgeons. They create a "thinking bypass" to replace feelings with thought and logic.
- Men tend to let women do their feeling for them.
- Men sometimes avoid situations and people who elicit certain feelings in them.
- Some men get sick or behave carelessly and hurt themselves so they have a reason to justify their feelings.[2]

People who are unaware of their emotions may also be out of touch with the sources of tension that overstimulate certain systems of the body. These can produce or aggravate such physical symptoms as ulcers, colitis, asthma, skin rashes, headaches, muscular aches, and tics. The bottom line in this—how a person deals with his emotions and feelings—determines to a great extent his (or her) physical, mental, and interpersonal health.

A Healthy View of Emotions

Men and women need to quit viewing feelings as enemies and see them as allies. What are the benefits of acknowledging and expressing our feelings?

> *Feelings motivate people.* They challenge us to do our best and assist us in some of our greatest accomplishments. Tapping into feelings is a tremendous energy source.
>
> *Feelings create a healthy environment.* Ignoring feelings depletes energy, whereas by expressing them, the air is cleared and we move on in life. We do not become stuck with excess baggage from the past. Expressing feelings is one of the best ways of reducing stress.
>
> *Feelings are the bridge to other people.* When we can trust our feelings and then in turn trust them to others, we build strong bonds of intimacy. Relating to others on the level of feelings means that we relate with them rather than at them.
>
> *When you express your feelings, you build self-confidence.* We tend to believe more in who we are and what we can do. We no longer have to live in fear of others discovering our feelings.
>
> *Feelings help us make the correct decisions.* Those who are in close touch with their feelings are more prepared to make difficult decisions and take important actions than those who are not.
>
> *Feelings help to heal both old and new wounds.* If you are hurt, you don't have to stay hurt. Feelings help us forgive others and also complete unfinished business.
>
> *Feelings give us life, since they are an endless source of fresh new energy.* They bring beauty into our souls.
>
> *Feelings and their expression give us another language with which to communicate with people and with God.*[3]

How do we begin to develop the language of feelings? The first and vital step is to develop a vocabulary of feeling words. One of the most practical ways to do this is to make a list of words you already are aware of for feelings and then take a resource such as *The Basic Book of Synonyms and Antonyms* and look up the various words. I looked up the word *fear* and found additional words such as *fright, dread, terror, alarm,* and *dismay.* The word *upset* can also be expressed as *disturb, agitate, fluster,* and *bother.*

Here are two different lists you can use as a resource. Once you have read through them, practice using them in sentences. Take one feeling and express it using some of the various words. When you share a response with someone else, attempt to use feeling words instead of expressing how you think. Remember that feelings are usually one- or two-word adjectives. If you give long dissertations such as "I feel that our government's position on Nicaragua is . . . ," those are thoughts, not feelings.

Here is a list of eight different words with their amplification.

HATE	FEAR	ANGER	HAPPINESS
1. dislike	1. fright	1. sore	1. joyful
2. bitter	2. terror	2. offended	2. enthusiastic
3. hateful	3. anxious	3. mad	3. merry
4. odious	4. misgivings	4. resentful	4. lucky
5. detest	5. concern	5. wrathful	5. fortunate
6. spiteful	6. harassed	6. hostile	6. pleased
7. aversion	7. dread	7. displeased	7. glad
8. despise	8. alarm	8. injured	8. satisfied
9. loathe	9. apprehension	9. vexed	9. contented
10. abominable	10. worry	10. torment	10. delighted

LOVE	DISAPPOINT-MENT	SADNESS	CONFUSION
1. affection	1. disturbed	1. tearful	1. mixed-up
2. loving	2. unhappy	2. grief	2. doubtful
3. amorous	3. unsatisfied	3. dejected	3. disorder
4. likable	4. frustrated	4. torment	4. bewilderment
5. tenderness	5. deluded	5. anguish	5. confounded
6. devotion	6. defeated	6. sorrow	6. disarray
7. attachment	7. hurt	7. unhappy	7. jumble
8. fondness	8. failure	8. gloomy	8. uncertain
9. passion	9. rejection	9. melancholy	9. perplexed
10. endearing	10. thwarted	10. mournful	10. embarrassment

Here is yet another list to help you learn the language of feelings. Notice there are words to describe your feelings when your wants are being satisfied and when they are not. In what situations would the words be appropriate, and when would they be inappropriate? With whom would you feel comfortable sharing these words? Check the feelings you can visualize yourself feeling and expressing. Select one and consider how you would express the word in a nonverbal manner.

When Wants Are Being Satisfied

absorbed	eager	grateful	peaceful
affection	elated	helpful	proud
alive	encouraged	inquisitive	radiant
amused	engrossed	inspired	refreshed
appreciation	enthusiastic	intense	relieved
astonished	excited	interested	secure
breathless	exhilarated	invigorated	spellbound
calm	expansive	jubilant	stimulated
cheerful	fascinated	keyed up	surprised
complacent	friendly	mellow	thrilled
concerned	fulfilled	merry	tranquil
confident	gleeful	moved	trust
curious	glowing	optimistic	wide awake
delighted	good-humored	overwhelmed	zestful

When Wants Are Not Satisfied

afraid	discouraged	hesitant	nettled
agitation	disgusted	horrible	passive
aloof	disheartened	hostile	perplexed
angry	dismayed	humdrum	provoked
animosity	disquieted	impatient	rancorous
annoyance	disturbed	inert	reluctant
anxious	downcast	infuriated	resentful
apprehensive	dread	insecure	restless
aversion	edgy	intense	scared
beat	embarrassed	irked	shaky
blah	exasperated	jealous	skeptical
bored	fatigued	jittery	sleepy
chagrined	fidgety	lassitude	sour
cold	frightened	let down	spiritless
confused	furious	listless	startled
cross	gloomy	lonely	suspicious
dejected	guilty	mean	thwarted
despondent	hate	miserable	troubled
detached	helpless	nervous	uneasy

It is important to learn your body's emotional signals. We all experience our emotions differently. For some, the feelings almost flood their bodies and overwhelm their rationality. For others, it means first thinking about what they feel, in order to become aware of the sensation. Still others experience their emotions first and then tune into their thoughts. Begin to express your emotions with a person you trust. This is a person who is not threatened by your expression and does not judge or criticize what you say. The person accepts you for who you are. When you do experience a feeling, share it as soon as possible, instead of letting it grow and even overwhelm you.

Once you begin to travel the road of expressing your feelings, you will not want to take detours, because the benefits are worth all the effort.

Remember:

Being emotionally handicapped is common and can be overcome.

God created us to experience emotions and feelings.

It takes less energy to experience and express our emotions than to hide them.

Feelings are our allies, not our enemies.

Build your vocabulary and then experiment sharing your new words.

By doing this, you will develop the flexibility to speak another language.

Energy Builders

1. What do we mean by the word *emotion?* What is the role of emotions in our lives? What does Scripture have to say about emotion? Who has the most difficulty in expressing feelings? Why?

2. How do people put up barriers to emotions? Have you used any of these? How can you begin to tear down any walls you've built?

3. What is the proper role of feelings in a healthy life? How can you make them your allies instead of your enemies?

4. Have you developed the language of feeling? Practice using some new words, if you need to. Does your language indicate that your wants have been satisfied? Are not satisfied?

5. How does your body react to emotions? Identify some of the signals it may be giving you.

6. What will you do this week with the information in this chapter? Describe how your communication will be different

Ten

The Language of Encouragement _____

Jan and Bill were seated in my office for the final session of premarital counseling. We had spent several hours together, and a good portion of the time was devoted to helping them improve their communication. Bill said to me, "Norm, we've spent a lot of time on communication, and I believe that Jan's and my communication *will* be different. I have one last question to ask you, though. If you were to suggest one principle of communication above all of the other important ones, what would it be?"

I didn't have to stop and think. I knew immediately.

"The principle is encouragement. When you communicate with others, use your verbal and nonverbal communication to encourage your partner or your friends or those with whom you work. We all need to be encouraged, but it is often a rare experience to find a positive, encouraging communicator."

What about you? Do you live in a citadel of encouragement or a castle of criticism? Do you hear encouragement each day, either coming from others or from yourself? If you were to make a list of what you say each day, would the column titled *encouragement* be longer than the *critical* list?

It is so easy to be a critic, but so rewarding to be an encourager.

Encouragement is the vital ingredient in personal and professional relationships. A person can be a brilliant doctor, a gifted teacher, a knowledgeable salesman, but if he or she lacks sensitivity, the person's other skills are hindered. When you encourage someone, you focus on the person's resources for the purpose of building that individual's self-esteem, self-confidence, and feelings of worth. You endeavor to build up that person as it states in 1 Thessalonians 5:11 (AMP), ". . . Encourage . . . edify . . . and build up—one another."

Who Is An Encourager?

You encourage by discovering the person's assets and reinforcing and noticing them. As you do this you redefine their liabilities and help people learn how to turn them into assets. By helping them discover untapped and as yet undiscovered resources, you uplift people.

The word *encourage* means "to give courage to." There are many occasions when people lack courage, and we need to loan them ours until theirs develops.

If you were to ask a group of individuals what it is like to be encouraged by another person and what they do to encourage others, you would find responses like the following:

> He understood my feelings.
> She listened to me and didn't judge me. She accepted where I was.
> Joanne responded to me as if I was a winner, a special person.
> I could be honest, and Mark wasn't shocked.
> I'll tell you why I felt encouraged. Mary had time for me.
> I really feel safe with Jim.
> Even when I didn't believe in myself and had no hope, Anne believed and, amazingly enough, had hope for herself and for me!
> My parents cheered me on in life.
> My best friend saw value in me as a person, even when I had a rotten day.

The list goes on and on.

How Can You Encourage Others?

How do you encourage others? By being able to find something of value to recognize when they are in despair. You focus on the effort or attempt the person makes in a difficult situation. Encouragers give courage not only through their words, but also through their nonverbals. An encouraging person is a total listener.

An encouraging person will use the following phrases frequently with others:

> You are a capable person.
> Give it a try.
> If you have made a mistake, you have learned. Mistakes are to learn from.
> Do it at your own pace and not mine.
> Give it your best shot.

Don Dinkmeyer and Lewis Losoncy suggest eight methods involved in the process of encouraging others.

Value the other person as he or she is. This means you believe the other person has resources within him that, though perhaps untapped, are available to help him meet life head-on. You do not focus on his weaknesses, but on his strong points.

In my counseling I work with many discouraged individuals. One of my goals as a counselor is to loan them my faith and belief in them until they have developed their own. People are quick to share their liabilities or perceived liabilities. I want to discover their assets, for their benefit and for the glory of God. We all need to be seen as God sees us—individuals of value and worth, to the extent that Jesus Christ died for us, to bring us back to God!

Often I ask the counselee to make a list of her assets and to share this list with herself each day until the list fully registers.

Another way of being an encourager is by *showing faith.* This means having confidence in another person, believing in the person even when there is little evidence that the person is believable. First Corinthians 13 says, "Love gives the other person the benefit of a doubt" (*see* v. 7). This type of encouragement may be hard for those of us who are very precise, detailed, and highly organized. We give someone a task; then we call in to check up on him. I don't think that being a "checker-upper" is a spiritual calling! Having faith means believing enough in the person not to call and check on him. That's risky! Your silence says, "I believe you can do it." In a family setting it can mean, "I believe you can make the right decision. Let me know *after* you've made your decision. I'm interested."

Building a person's *self-respect* is another way of being an encourager. One way to do this is to help the person become aware of her resources. Another way is by giving him compliments that are not always based upon his accomplishments or performance.

You can be an encourager by *recognizing effort and im-*

provement. This lets others know they are acceptable as they are, not only as they could be. Too often with children, spouses, and in business we emphasize the completed task. This communicates to others that they are acceptable only as they become perfect.

You can be an encourager by *recognizing and focusing on strengths and assets.* I think we have been conditioned to point out people's mistakes and liabilities. But living in a mistake-oriented environment is not very pleasant. As you consider the people in your own family, which is easier for you to complete: a list of ten of their strengths and assets or a list of ten of their weaknesses? Identify people's strengths, focus on them, and build them. But you have to be an encourager to yourself first, if you're going to be able to encourage others.

Identifying resources in others and helping them develop them is a sign of an encourager. A talent scout sees the undeveloped potential in a person and becomes an enabler to that individual. As an encourager you respond to the person's raw material, not the finished product. But to do this you need to look past the person's present performance and invest in him. Who have you invested in recently? How did you share your observations and vision with the person?[1]

Recently some friends of ours shared an experience of their son's with us. He is about eleven years of age and has been taking piano lessons for several years. Recently he played in their church's evening service, and the music director of the church heard his performance. Afterwards he came up to the parents and said, "Your son has tremendous potential. I'd like to give him lessons every other week and help him develop that potential. Someday our capable pianist here at the church will move on, and we need to prepare for that time. Your son could become the next pianist." This encouragement came from a very famous choir director in one of the largest churches in California.

Throughout the world, people are starving for positive

feedback and positive statements. Compliments and appreciation feel good to both the sender and the receiver.

How Can You Discourage Others?

Are you aware of some of the ways in which you might discourage others? Consider these methods of discouragement, which all of us are guilty of from time to time.

Overprotection is a very common approach. We may overprotect for the "good of the person," but unfortunately it robs him of freedom and initiative. When a person is hovered over in this manner, he ends up feeling ineffective and inferior.

Silence may subtly but devastatingly discourage people. By taking them for granted or failing to notice their efforts or progress, we may tell them they are doing something unacceptable. Often others view lack of freedom as negative feedback. All of us need recognition!

Intimidation is another way of discouraging others. How could you do this? By not responding to a person's style of communication or ignoring what she says and moving ahead as though she had never said anything. We can also intimidate by having an unrealistic standard of perfection. In the other person this creates the belief, *I can never measure up, so why try!* I have come in contact with some people with whom, very honestly, I would rather not spend time talking. They play the game "Can You Top This?" If you share an experience or accomplishment, they immediately tell of their own act as though they had never even heard what you said.

Consider the following words that encourage and discourage. Do any of them sound familiar?

Words That Encourage	*Words That Discourage*
Knowing you, I'm sure that you will do fine.	Knowing you, I think that you should do more.
You can make it.	You usually make mistakes, so be careful.

Words That Encourage	Words That Discourage
I have faith in you.	I doubt that you can do it.
Thanks for your help.	If you had finished clearing the table, that would have been helpful.
You're doing fine.	You can do better.
I enjoyed that song.	Your music is getting better, but you missed the notes at the end.
I can see you put a lot of effort into that.	That is a good job, but the corners are ragged.
You have really improved.	Well, you're playing a little better than last year.
You'll figure it out.	You had better get some help. That looks very difficult.
You can only learn by trying.	I doubt you should try.
That was a good effort. Don't worry about the mistake.	Why didn't you think of that before you started?
Let's think this through together.	How can you be so dumb?
You've done some good thinking. Are you ready to start?	That plan will never work.
That's a challenge. But I'm sure you'll make it.	That is too difficult for you. I'll do it.[2]

Perhaps you've heard about two types of people: basement people and balcony people. Basement people live in a dark, damp basement and are lurking there, waiting for you to walk by. When you do, they leap up, grab you, and pull you down into that basement. These people are our critics, and their joy in life is to tear us down and maim us.

Balcony people on the other hand, lean over the balcony as you walk by and say, "Go for it, I'm for you. You can do it. I'm with you. I'm praying for you. I'm behind you. Give it a try." They encourage us!

If you want to build your relationships with others, become a balcony person. You will relate more with others by focusing on their strengths and what they do right than on their weaknesses and what they do wrong.

As you relate to people in your life at work, home, and church think of those people as gifts whom God has entrusted to you. He wants you to respond as a helper and not as a hindrance. They are there to receive your affirmation. Become a treasure seeker and begin to prospect other people's lives. Look for their beliefs, attitudes, abilities, and hidden talents that need to be affirmed. Perhaps all of us, including myself, could use some training as a talent scout. Perhaps all of us need to change the prescription in our glasses from time to time as we view other people. Our perception may become blurred and fuzzy.

As we are reminded to encourage others, remember to encourage yourself. Why not affirm yourself? God does! The verse, "Encourage . . . edify . . . and build up—one another" applies to others and to you!

Energy Builders

1. Make an encouragement list and a critical list for the things you hear in a day. Make another for the things you say. What can you learn from each?

2. How can you encourage other people? Yourself? What words or phrases could you use? Are they a part of your regular vocabulary? What methods can you use to encourage others?

3. What kind of statements discourage you? What kind encourage you? Which do you use most often when you talk to others?

4. What is a *basement person*? A *balcony person*? How have you been each? Who has been each to you? What do you admire about the balcony people in your life? List some ways you could become a balcony person this week.

5. What will you do this week with the information in this chapter? Describe how your communication will be different.

Eleven

The Second Most Important Conversation— With Ourselves _____

Do you talk to yourself? It's all right to admit that you do. It doesn't mean that your chimney is missing a brick or your elevator doesn't go to the top floor. We all talk to ourselves. It's normal. We carry on inner dialogues all day long. Sometimes they are actual conversations, or they may simply be a series of beliefs we cling to and that we tell ourselves regularly. Our inner dialogues reflect our beliefs and attitudes about ourselves, others, our experiences, the past, the future, God, and so on.

Did you know that:

> What you express in your outer dialogue with others is a reflection of the inner dialogue you carry on with yourself.
> How you behave toward others is determined by your inner dialogue, not by their behaviors or responses.
> Most of your emotions—such as anger, depression, guilt, worry—are initiated and escalated by your self-talk.

As you sit in church on Sunday morning are you aware of how many conversations are occurring during the minister's sermon? You say, "There are no conversations. The pastor is preaching, and the people in the sanctuary sit there and listen." Right? Wrong! Some people are listening, but many of them are miles away, engrossed in their own thoughts and inner conversations Even as you look around and note the apparent rapt attention, you might be amazed to discover how many people are actually talking to themselves. The person next to you might be rehearsing what he is going to say to his employee at work the next day. The next person over may be formulating what she is going to say to her teenager, who is sitting two rows up with her friends and talking back and forth, disturbing others around them. The lady next to you who is smiling and looking attentively at the minister may be thinking, *Oh, I should never have come this morning. I just know George is upset with me again. Nothing, absolutely nothing has gone right lately. I wish this depression would go away. I just know something is wrong the way George has been acting. I wonder if other people can tell how I feel? Why did the minister choose to preach on that subject today? Doesn't he know what that does to me? I wish this service would get over so I could talk to George.* Inner dialogue such as that may not surprise us. Why? Because most of us have done the very same thing.

Lloyd Ogilvie says, "Actually, a constant flow of dialogue takes place inside us while we are talking to other people. We talk over in the private chamber of our minds what we think the other person is saying, what's really meant beneath the words, or how we are going to respond once he or she stops talking. Sometimes we actually say within ourselves what we are going to say or what we'd really like to say if we dared."[1]

What Do You Say to Yourself?

Most people do not realize the tremendous power and effect of their inner dialogue. *Our internal thoughts determine what we do and say!* This means that what I have said in the previous chapters is dependent upon what is said in this chapter. You can attempt to listen with your ears and your eyes, pace another individual, match that person's tempo, inflection, and words, and even use words that reflect the person's vocabulary. But the effectiveness of this will be determined by your inner dialogue. Is that powerful!

Wouldn't it be fascinating to have a computer printout of your own inner dialogue for just a day? Most of us would be shocked by what that printout would reveal. You know what? We might be shocked to note some of the differences between what we say to ourselves about ourselves in our inner dialogue and what we say to others in our outward conversation. Many people talk to others quite differently from the way they talk to themselves.

What do I mean? Over the years I have discovered that many people talk in a polite, concerned, interested, and objective manner to others, but they do not treat themselves with the same regard. They respond objectively to others, but talk to themselves in an unrealistic, self-depreciating way that can bring on depression, low self-esteem, worry, and anger. These emotions in turn will affect what we say to others and how objectively we listen and respond.

Automatic Thinking

Many of our thoughts are automatic. They jump into our consciousnesses without any planning or conscious prompting. Let's consider the characteristics of automatic thoughts.

First of all, an automatic thought is a specific message. A young woman who is afraid of being rejected by men tells herself, *He isn't interested in me. I'm not attractive enough.* This thought affects her verbal and nonverbal responses with that man. She may act hesitant and ill at ease and bring about the very rejection she fears. Or she may overcompensate by appearing overly confident and self-assured and push him away.

Often an automatic thought surfaces, not necessarily in complete form, but in a shorthand manner. It may take the form of a visual image or just a few words. The automatic thought may be a brief memory of something that occurred in the past, or it could be a series of disconnected words. A word or a series of short telegraphic phrases may serve as a label or summary for an entire group of painful memories, fears, or self-degrading statements.

Usually we believe our automatic thoughts, regardless of how irrational or off-the-wall they appear. They may appear rational because we very rarely check them out or verify them. Because we fail to test them, and the more they occur, the more we believe them.

We experience these thoughts spontaneously. They just pop into our minds and, since they're there, why shouldn't they be true.

Another characteristic of automatic thoughts is that they include the terminology of *must, should,* or *ought.* We call these "torture words," since they elevate guilt and lower self-esteem. "I *should* do this . . . ," or, "I *must* be a perfect mother . . . ," or, "I *ought* to be consistent and never make a mistake." When these words appear on the screen of our minds, they generate hopelessness.

Automatic thoughts have the unique characteristic of "awfulizing." These thoughts expect the worst, see the danger behind every bush, and create intense anxiety. They can color our attitude for days and undermine healthy communication.

We can also find automatic thoughts difficult to stop. They

may appear somewhat reasonable, and since they just pop in, they may become camouflaged amidst our other thoughts. Since they tend to come and go at will, it's hard to put a leash on them.

You learn your automatic thoughts by listening to other people and what they've said about you. Then you believe those statements.

Distorted Thinking

Distorted thinking comes in many packages. To begin to counter and eventually eliminate it, first we must identify such thoughts. Our goal is to break free from being a captive of our thoughts by bringing every thought captive under Christ. Let's consider the various distortions.

1. *Filtering* can distort our thoughts. Another name for this is *tunnel vision*. A person looks at one element of a situation, while ignoring everything else. Your listening is highly selective. For example, you might receive praise from your boss for a project you just completed. But at the same time he gives you a constructive, positive suggestion for the next project. Which do you dwell upon? Some would concentrate on the suggestion, reinterpret it, and see it as a negative statement. A person may then tend to both magnify and awfulize the statement. Then he will exaggerate his fears, losses, and irritations, thus hindering his communication. We all have our own tunnels. Some of us, for instance, are sensitive to anything that hints at loss, making us the center of attention, or frustration. When any of these occur, they activate our filtering tape.

2. *Polarized thinking* is another way we distort things. This means you tend to see everything in extremes and leave no room for a middle ground. People are either bad or good. Thus if a person makes one mistake, he judges himself as imperfect, a loser, no good. One mistake and "it's all over."

3. Another frequent distortion is *overgeneralization*, in which a conclusion is based on one incident or piece of evidence. A young man asks a girl out and is turned down. He

thinks, *I'll never be able to get a date.* If you eat clams one time and become ill, you say, *I'll never be able to eat clams again.* If her spouse breaks a promise, a wife thinks, *I'll never be able to trust him again.* One bad experience means that in a similar situation, you can expect a repeat.

Absolute statements characterize overgeneralizations, "No one appreciates a thing I do"; "I'll never be able to get this right"; "I guess I'll always be depressed!" "Nobody likes me anymore." You ignore evidence to the contrary.

4. *Mind reading*—making snap judgments about situations or people—creates distortions. Although we have no evidence for something, we believe in the decision of a moment. Assumptions are made based on hunches, intuition, one or two past experiences, or some vague feelings.

The Smith family didn't greet me after church because they didn't like my message. Or, *I just know they don't want to come, so why invite them?* The conclusions are made and set in concrete rather than being checked out.

5. *Catastrophizing* means making a mountain out of a molehill. Such thinking frequently begins with the words *what if. . . ?* This is the cry of the worrier. One small problem means a disaster is on the way. A car is stolen a half mile away: *What if ours is stolen . . . ?* The person continues to talk to himself, along these lines, amplifying the situation, making it larger and larger.

6. *Personalization* is the distortion of relating everything to you. If a family member is sad, you blame yourself. If another person feels hurt, you take the responsibility, whether or not you were involved Your spouse makes the angry statement, "I wish people were more considerate . . . ," and immediately you believe she is talking about you.

Comparison with others is a main feature of this distortion. *He is a better speaker than I am, I'm the most ineffective minister in town, I'm not of the same caliber as the rest of those people.* You base your value upon a comparison with others. Each comparison has an effect upon your perception of your own value and worth.

7. *Emotional reasoning* is a very common distortion. If you feel something, it must be true. If you feel like a failure, you must be a failure. If you feel guilty, you must have violated your standards. All negative things you feel about life, others, and yourself must be true. Why? Because you feel them. These feelings come from distorted thoughts, and they in turn reinforce the thoughts. The distorted pattern of thinking and feelings can be the biggest deceiver a person has to contend with.

8. *Blaming* brings us relief and also distorted thinking. It's nice to know that someone is responsible—especially someone else. In blaming, we see others as responsible and ease our own culpability. If your feelings are hurt, someone else is responsible. If you're afraid, someone else caused those feelings.

Others walk through life as blame collectors. They have an incessant need to be wrong.

9. *Shoulds* are very common distortions. A person who often falls into this trap operates with a set of very inflexible rules that he sees as correct, indisputable, and absolute; he also believes any deviation from those rules is bad. Other people should "know this" or "do this." They should be a certain way, think a certain way. *Shoulds* are a form of self-inflicted suffering and pain, a form of emotional masochism.

10. *The need to always be right* leads to a constant pattern of defensiveness and distorted thinking. It requires expending consistent effort to prove that your perspective is *always* right. Others' opinions don't count, and you do not even hear them. You never make mistakes, thus are impossible to live with.[2]

Have you experienced these ten kinds of distorted thinking? If so, how did it affect your communication? Which ones have you used most often?

I have spent many hours counseling clients about getting control of their inner dialogues. As we begin to identify the relationship between what is happening in their relationships with other people and their inner dialogues, one of their first questions is "what do I do to change?" I answer, quite simply, "Become aware of your inner dialogues." But the application of this principle takes conscious effort and consistency. To bring your thinking into balance and develop objectivity, you must begin to become aware of the kinds of thoughts you experience in specific situations. It's almost as though several times a day, you need to shout to yourself, "PAY ATTENTION! LISTEN TO YOURSELF!"

How to Alter Your Thinking

At first it is not so easy to stop what you are doing or experiencing and begin to think about what you think. If you experience anger, anxiety, depression, or a feeling of rejection, it becomes difficult to take yourself away from your feeling, to look at your thoughts. But you *can* learn to do it! many people have. And their lives and communication have changed. Practice makes the difference.

What Do You Think?

The first step is to *identify your thoughts.* Think of a situation from the past week that you believe you didn't handle too well, for one reason or another. Try to recall what you were thinking before and during the time when things didn't go well for you. Recall your actual inner dialogue. You don't have to come up with the identical words, but those that reflect what you were thinking. If you have difficulty recalling the words, what were you feeling at that time? Just try to come up with some specific words to identify your feeling.

Start with, "I felt . . . ," and then finish the sentence. Some people find it helpful to write out "I felt" several times and complete each one. After you identify the feeling, it will be easier to reconstruct the inner thoughts or dialogue. You may discover that some of your dialogue was about a person, the situation, or even the feelings you were experiencing.

After you have identified your feelings and thoughts, try to recall what you actually said in your conversation with others. What would you have preferred saying? What types of thoughts or inner dialogue would you have needed in order to say what you wanted to say? That is one of the key principles to follow to enhance your communication with others. In order to listen in the way you want to listen and in order to communicate in the manner you want to with others, *identify what you need to say to yourself for this to happen.*

Dissect and Reassemble Your Thoughts

In order to change your pattern of thinking, next you'll need to *dissect and reassemble* your thinking. This simply means assessing your thoughts and changing them. Before you are engaged in a conversation or interaction with another person or during the interchange itself decide what you need to alter. Your brain works quite fast, and you *can* quickly think about what you are thinking without distracting yourself too much.

But hold it a minute! Doesn't this contradict the principles of effective listening I've just outlined? Yes and no. With concentration we can listen to ourselves and others at the same time. In fact, in order to become total listeners, we need to do both. We have to clear up our own inner static, which already interferes with the sending, transmission, and receiving of the message.

One way to think on your feet is to give yourself permission to take time to think and not respond immediately to the other person. Somehow we have accepted the myth that we must always be capable of responding immediately, even if we are not ready to do so. As you begin to slow down you will soon begin to develop a greater proficiency and will quickly recognize your inner dialogue. You will be able to identify what is accurate and what is inaccurate and be able to reassemble it.

If you have a particularly stressful situation facing you in the future, benefit from having advance practice. It will prepare you for the encounter, thus reducing stress and making communication more effective.

Here is an example of a person who identified the situation that upset him and then analyzed his thoughts. You might try doing the same thing.

Situation

(Briefly describe the undesirable situation which upsets you.)

I can't live in an apartment with two other friends my first year of college, because my parents won't allow it.

Inner Dialogue

(Identify what you tell yourself when you think about this unfair and undesirable situation. *Dissect!*)

1. This is awful.

2. This is unfair.

3. My parents are just trying to control me, and they don't trust me.

4. My friends will find someone else to room with, and then I won't ever get to be with them in an apartment.

Correct analysis of the situation

(This is done to determine whether the description you have given of your situation is accurate.)

The situation is true. They won't let me move, and if I were to do so, my support would be cut off.

Reassemble

(This is the time to challenge the truth and helpfulness of each item of self-talk and reassemble statements that would accurately describe the meaning of your situation and be in your own best interest to believe.)

1. Where is the evidence that this is awful? It is disappointing, but it is not the end of the world. I have handled other disappointments before. I may discover later on that moving wouldn't have worked out.

2. What is unfair about it? That depends on how I interpret it. Fairness is not the issue here.

3. How do I know that my parents are trying to control me? That's mind reading. Have I asked them if that is their purpose? They have trusted me many times and have given me freedom. I can write down the reasons they gave me for not moving in with my friends.

4. How do I know my friends will find someone else? What if they do? Does that mean they are no longer my friends? Where is the evidence that I will never get to be with them? I am feeling sorry for myself and looking at the worst consequences.

Inner Dialogue	Reassemble
5. I always miss out on good times like that.	5. I don't always miss out. I have lots of good times. I am allowing this one disappointment to erase all of my memories of good times. I can list some of them.

How might that student have communicated with his parents if he had followed the statements in the first column? He might have sulked or pouted, become angry, withdrawn, overreacted to his parents, felt sorry for himself, and acted like a martyr. The responses in the second column are objective, adult responses that will affect both the emotions and the communication.

In the next chapter we will look in more depth at some ways to prepare our thoughts ahead of time when we face difficult situations.

Remember:

**Identify your thoughts.
Dissect and reassemble them.**

Energy Builders

1. Why are the thoughts you communicate to yourself so important? How do they affect you? Others? How do they influence what you say and do?

2. Try to keep track of your automatic thinking for a day or two. At the end of that time, have you learned anything surprising about yourself? What was it?

3. How have you allowed automatic thoughts to influence you? Have some of them been based on distorted thinking? If so, which kind of distorted thinking do you find yourself caught in most often? Are there other kinds you also use frequently?

4. In order to begin to take control of your automatic thoughts, begin to identify them. Think of a situation you

didn't handle too well and recall your inner dialogue and feelings. What did you say to others? How can you change your inner dialogue to communicate in a better way? Dissect and reorganize your thinking in this situation. Reassemble it to show yourself a clearer picture of what really went on.

5. What will you do this week with the information in this chapter? Describe how your communication will be different.

Twelve

Taking Control of Your Thought Life _____

Jim had worked for the same company for four years but had not yet received a raise. Although he felt his work was more than adequate, he had hesitated to ask for money because he feared confrontations and facing negative reactions from others. He liked things peaceful and harmonious. Finally Jim decided it was time to take some action. He identified what he wanted to say and practiced expressing it in line with his boss's communication style.

As he walked into his boss's office, Jim began to feel a bit anxious. First his stomach started to churn. When this occurred, he said to himself, *All right, I can handle this. I have prepared for it.* After a few preliminaries, Jim's boss asked if there was something he wanted to talk about.

When he heard this, Jim felt his stomach tie up in a knot. He quickly countered these feelings with a *self-instructional* statement. *All right. I do feel tense; take a deep breath. I don't have to be concerned how I make this request. It will come out all right.* He felt better as soon as he shared with his boss that he wanted to talk about a raise.

As they continued to discuss the possibility, Jim's tension rose and subsided from time to time. Whenever it began to rise, he gave himself another instructional message. He would tell himself things like, *You're doing fine. Just slow down a bit and see yourself being calm.* When the tension subsided, he reinforced himself by saying, *Ah, I knew I could do it. That's better.* They talked for a while, and the discussion ended with Jim's employer saying he would consider the request and get back to him.

Jim left the office feeling quite tense. As he returned to his office the tension increased. *Now, why am I feeling upset?* he asked himself. He realized that he was making some *should* statements to himself. *I should have had an answer before I left. I should have pushed for an answer. Perhaps I didn't present it properly. I could have done better.* Then he began to counter these statements with more positive statements. He gave himself permission to feel a bit disappointed over the delay. In asking, he had taken a major step, he told himself. He had taken the initiative, and regardless of the outcome, he'd made progress. The next time he asked for a raise, he'd find it easier. Even though he hadn't gotten an immediate answer, he *had* handled himself well in the meeting. Several times during the day Jim reinforced himself this way, and by evening he felt good about his progress.

Taking Control in Difficult Situations

Perhaps you identify with an experience such as Jim's. You may have had a tense encounter with an employee, a family member, or a friend, or maybe you felt unsure of yourself in a class setting or in joining a new organization.

We all face situations that provoke anxiety, tension, or stress. Unfortunately most of us prepare for these encounters in such a manner that we create even more tension for ourselves: We anticipate the worst and spend time talking to ourselves in a negative, defeating manner. I'd like to show you a better way. By *identifying, analyzing,* and *reassembling* your thoughts, you can more successfully communicate in difficult situations and control a situation that once controlled you.

Jim used some of the ideas I want to present to you. In advance he had *identified* a cue (his stomach churning) that would remind him to use the self-instructional statement he had already thought out. In the past this cue would have elicited anxious, worrisome thoughts, and his emotional reaction would have intensified. He had already *analyzed* the situation ahead of time, though, because he had developed some inner-dialogue statements to use. Finally Jim praised himself when he found his statements working.

Now let's see how these and other guidelines can work effectively in various situations.

When You Deal With Anger

I think many people would agree that a situation involving anger is very difficult to deal with. Most of us find it one of the hardest times to continue to communicate clearly and rationally. Whether the anger comes from ourselves or someone else, we need to prepare carefully for our reactions. Here I'd like to suggest an approach based on the steps Jim took.

1. Prepare Yourself Mentally.   By using a rational and sane inner dialogue with yourself before you come into the situation, you can make yourself ready for an encounter with another individual. Work out guiding statements such as these:

> What is the best approach for me to take with this person?
> This discussion may upset me, but I think I know what to say.
>
> From my perspective, there is no need to argue, raise my voice, or become angry.
>
> I don't fully know the person's perspective, and she may become upset. That is all right, because I can handle it. I don't need to become upset and allow my emotions to be controlled by the other person.
>
> I can try not to take this too seriously.
>
> I will relax, take a deep breath, and visualize myself staying calm in this discussion.
>
> I will remember to listen to the other person, and I do not have to respond immediately. In fact, it may be helpful to ask a question before responding.

Such thoughts will encourage you to keep your self-control, even if others do not. As you follow them, you will set the tone for your conversation.

2. Think About Inner Dialogue Beforehand. Prepare inner-dialogue statements to use during the conversation, in case your feelings begin to build up. You might tell yourself:

> My muscles are beginning to tighten up. It's time to relax and slow down.
>
> I feel the other person's anger, and I am beginning to feel mine. It is all right for the other person to be angry. In fact, I give that person permission to be angry. I need to listen to him at this time.
>
> This is a good opportunity for me to practice what Proverbs states in several verses, "Be slow to anger." In fact, by being slow to anger, I may not become angry at all.
>
> I need to remember that her anger reflects the fact that she is hurt, afraid, or frustrated.
>
> It may help us to take these issues point by point.
>
> Maybe we are both right.
>
> I want to work constructively with this person.
>
> It would help me to look for the positives in this situation.

These are examples of different types of statements a person can use when emotions begin to rise. Identify the ones you would find most helpful. If you would not like to use any of these, make up some of your own. Then practice them and review them prior to identifiable problem encounters.

3. *Take Your Reaction Into Account.* Plan for your reaction following a difficult time. Some of our encounters go quite well and others do not. Often we talk to ourselves following the situation, and our inner dialogue can either be upsetting or comforting. I've listed some examples of self-affirming statements. Select those you think would be helpful or develop your own.

> That was a difficult situation, and it takes time to work through the issues.
> I don't have to take what was said personally.
> It would be helpful for me to write down what she said and then evaluate its accuracy tomorrow. It might be important to see it from her point of view.
> That was not as difficult as I anticipated.
> I handled that fairly well. I am improving from what I used to do.
> I feel I can be pleased with the progress I made[1]

If you use these steps, with practice you will find yourself dealing with highly emotional situations in a sensible, organized fashion that will benefit you and those with whom you communicate.

When You Deal With Rejection

We've all had times when we've felt unwanted. Maybe our parents or other relatives didn't treat us well in a situation. Or perhaps we never did well in athletics, and when teams chose players at school, we were always the last to get picked; even then our newfound team didn't seem too happy to have us. Whenever we've run into it, we've felt the pain of rejection, and we do our utmost to avoid it.

Many people live in constant fear of being rejected. Even for those who don't, entering into a new situation with new people carries with it the hint of that fear—the fear of not being accepted or liked or not making a good impression. When this is present, no matter to what degree, our inner dialogue can either help us or hinder us; it can lessen the threat or heighten it; it can help us be either accepted or rejected.

With new people we ask ourselves, *Will they like me? Will they speak to me and show an interest in me?* Such questions set us up for not being able to communicate effectively with them. But it doesn't have to be that way. Let me use the example of rejection to share four basic steps we can use with other situations as well.

1. Whatever the Situation, Analyze What You Say to Yourself. Let's assume you are sitting in an office, waiting for an appointment. You have just started a conversation with another person. That individual listens for a minute, makes a few responses, and returns to reading his magazine. You try again, but receive a minimal response. What occurs in your inner dialogue? Do you make negative comments about yourself? Do you make negative comments about the other individual? Do you use labels such as *rude person,* or do you say to yourself, *I'm a poor conversationalist?* Try to identify negative statements and labels you use in situations such as these. Begin to eliminate the negative labels and simply describe the situation objectively. *I made an attempt at a conversation, and for some reason the other person did not wish to continue it.* That is objective, and you do not blame yourself or the other person involved.

2. Reframe What You Say to Yourself in Advance. Reframing is simply giving another interpretation to a potential or actual situation. When we have a fear of rejection or even have anxiety over a new situation, it is largely because of how we conceptualize or frame our initial encounter with the person or event. We use statements like:

> They may not like me.
> I'm afraid I won't say what I want to, and I will make a bad impression.

He probably won't be interested in me as a person.

They probably think I'm a pest, and they may be rude to me.

What do statements like this accomplish? They set us up for failure and anticipation of the worst. We actually enter into the new situation at a disadvantage!

Become aware of your negative thinking. Take a look at what you say to yourself ahead of time and recast it in a positive tone. Instead of dwelling on the possibility for failure tell yourself:

They'll think I'm great!

I've checked and double-checked what I want to say, and I'm ready for them.

He's probably more interested in me than I'd guessed.

They seem like very nice people; they shouldn't say anything bad to me.

Give the best interpretation to your situations, and you'll set yourself up for success!

3. Reframe Your Responses During Your Interaction With Others. If you meet someone new or are involved with a new group of people, and they do not appear interested in you or in what you have to offer or sell, you can interpret this in a variety of ways. You can see yourself as inadequate and unworthy. You can look for defects in how you look or in your social communication skills. Or you can consider the hundreds of reasons for what took place.

Let's say you ask a person who is new in your church to join you for lunch after a service, and that person turns you down. What do you say about yourself? Some people would conduct mental, unconstructive surgery upon themselves. In place of this, make a list of twenty reasons why *you* might refuse a lunch invitation after church. Then consider your list. Do these reasons reflect upon the person who invited you or more upon what is taking place in your life at that moment? Whenever you find yourself turned down for some request, in place of mind reading, assuming a defect within yourself, or becoming irritated at the other person, make a list, and you will find a multitude of excellent reasons.

4. Before Engaging in a New Experience, Rehearse and Visualize What You Would Like to Say and How You Would Like to Say It. Anticipate and plan for what you will say if the outcome is not as you wanted. In advance bring a balance into your inner dialogue.

Taking Control in a Positive Situation

Not only does our inner dialogue influence how we communicate with others in difficult situations, it also affects how we both give and receive pleasant messages. In fact it can actually control how much praise we give and receive and how we react to the compliments people give us.

Inner Dialogue and Giving Compliments. Already we've seen the importance of encouragement and compliments, but how often have you wanted to say something like this to another person, yet halted before the words left your lips? Negative (or dysfunctional) thoughts like the ones listed in the chart below may have prevented you from saying what you really felt.

Praise Thought	*Dysfunctional Thought*
John's a really terrific student. He's the best in the class and seems to have a real knack for learning.	Everyone's always telling him how good he is, and he always gets top grades. He doesn't need to hear anything like that from me.
I'm just crazy about Lisa. She does all kinds of things that make me love her more every day.	I've told her I love her. Why should I tell her again?
Doug does the best job of selling in the whole company. He really deserves all the closings he's made.	If I told him something like that, he might not like it. Maybe he'd feel embarrassed.

Praise Thought	Dysfunctional Thought
Andrea is a great kid. I'm proud she's my granddaughter. I'd like to tell the pastor how much his ministry means to me. He's such a good preacher, too.	She'll just think the old man's goofy. I'll look so foolish! I won't say it right to him. I wouldn't even know how to start, because I'd feel so embarrassed.
Jane's the nicest girl in my class. I'd like to date her.	I think she's really great, but she may not be interested in me at all.
Sam's so good at woodworking. I really liked that piece he sold to Mrs. Miller. I wonder if he'd teach me how to do it?	I'm not that good at doing things like that. He'd just laugh at me.

By falling prey to such negative thoughts, you have lost an opportunity to say some words that might have pleased another person. In all likelihood the assumptions you made were not at all valid, but they kept you from employing the language of encouragement.

Inner Dialogue and Receiving Praise. On the other hand, how often have you received compliments, then talked yourself out of them in your inner (or even your outer) dialogue? Maybe you've heard praise like that below and had the parallel response in your inner dialogue.

Praise or Compliment	Dysfunctional Thoughts
You've really done a good job.	All he cares about is what I do. He doesn't really care about me.
You have great potential.	I'm tired of hearing about my potential. What do they like about me right now?
You're a very attractive person.	I don't feel attractive. I look dumpy, and this is an old outfit. I wonder who she's trying to kid? I wonder what she wants?

These inner statements can lead to various reactions that affect our relationships with others. Eventually the well of compliments may run dry. Look at how some of our negative responses can make the compliment giver feel:

> Some people *deny* compliments. "Oh, me! That wasn't really that much. Anyone here could have done that." After hearing that, the other person may feel sorry that she said anything in the first place!
>
> Other people *reject* the compliments. "I can't believe you like this suit, I've worn it for years, and it's actually a bit frayed. The truth is I look a mess today." When he hears this, the other person is bound to feel you think his opinion valueless. Yet we do this to friends and even to our spouses!
>
> *Sarcasm* is another response. "Oh, sure, I look great. Where did you get your taste?" Such a response puts other people down.

Words like these may reflect that the person saying them has trouble with his or her self-esteem. That individual needs to develop a better way to respond to the positive messages we all deeply want.

How can we change the way we respond? When we hear ourselves answering praise with negative inner dialogue, we need to counter that with factual statements that more accurately describe the situation. This will help us to change our inner thoughts and take control of the situation. As we respond positively to praise we will hear more of it, because people will know it will be well received. What a boost to self-esteem!

Response to Inner Dialogue

How can we answer our inner dialogue when we hear those thoughts? Let's take a look at the charts we've seen earlier in this chapter to get an idea of how thoughts about giving and receiving praise might be checked for accuracy.

When you begin to identify your negative thinking and take control of it, you can begin to see the change in your automatic thoughts and reactions. Soon you will feel the freedom to give and receive praise in a positive way.

Inner Dialogue and Compliments

Praise Thought	Dysfunctional Thought	More Accurate Thoughts
John's a really terrific student. He is the best in the class and seems to have a real knack for learning.	Everyone's always telling him how good he is, and he always gets top grades. He doesn't need to hear anything like that from me.	Even if he does know it, he may not know *you* recognize how good he is and admire him for it. Others might feel jealous.
I'm just crazy about Lisa. She does all kinds of things that make me love her more day by day.	I've told her I love her. Why should I tell her again?	She'll like hearing that again. Then she'll know you still love her and that your love is growing.
Doug does the best job of selling in the whole company. He really deserves all the closings he's made.	If I told him something like that, he might not like it. Maybe he'd feel embarrassed.	Maybe he'll feel embarrassed for a few minutes, but he'll have heard the praise and feel good about it later.
Andrea is a great kid. I'm proud that she's my granddaughter.	She'll just think the old man's goofy. I'll look so foolish.	You'll show her how much you really do care. She'll appreciate your love.

I'd like to tell the pastor how much his ministry means to me. He's such a good preacher, too.

Jane's the nicest girl in my class. I'd like to date her.

Sam's so good at woodworking. I really liked that piece he sold to Mrs. Miller. I wonder if he'd teach me how to do it?

I won't say it right to him. I wouldn't even know how to start, because I'd feel so embarrassed.

I think she's really great, but she may not be interested in me at all.

I'm not good at doing things like that. He'd just laugh at me.

What you say doesn't have to be perfect. Just be sincere, and your appreciation will show.

You can both accept that you might not feel the same about each other. When you've talked to her she seemed friendly, so she might like you, too.

I'd have to start to learn before I know if I'd be any good at it. If he laughs at me, I can tell him how uncomfortable it makes me feel.

Inner Dialogue and Praise

Praise or Compliment	*Dysfunctional Thoughts*	*More Accurate Thoughts*
You've really done a good job.	All he cares about is what I do. He doesn't really care about me.	He always asks me how things are going. We have a friendly relationship most of the time. The pressure on this project has just gotten to me today.
You have great potential.	I'm tired of hearing about my potential. What do they like about me right now?	They're saying they have faith in me. They think I can do even more in the future, and that feels good.
You're a very attractive person.	I don't feel attractive. I look dumpy, and this is an old outfit. I wonder who she is trying to kid? I wonder what she wants?	It's nice to know someone likes the way I look, even if I don't *feel* great. What I look like on one day doesn't necessarily influence how she sees me all the time. She doesn't have to want something to say a kind word to me. She's never done that before.

Inner Dialogue Evaluation

To help yourself accurately identify the thoughts you need to change and how you need to reframe them, ask yourself the following questions. We all fall into these traps at some point, and it may take just a few questions to identify your negative thinking. Once you've done that, you're only one step away from changing it.

1. What Is the Evidence? Ask yourself, *Would this thought hold up in a court of law? Is it circumstantial evidence?* Just because your mailman misses delivering the mail one day does not mean that you cannot count on anything. Just because you tripped walking into your new class and everyone laughed does not mean that you will trip again or that they think you are a clod.

2. Am I Making a Mistake in Assuming What Causes What? It is often difficult to determine causes. Many people worry about their weight, and if they gain weight they make the assumption, *I don't have any willpower.* But is that the only reason? Could there be other causes such as glandular imbalance, using eating as a means to deal with unhappiness, and so on? We do not know the causes of obesity for certain. The medical profession is still studying the problem.

3. Am I Confusing a Thought With a Fact? Do you say, *I've failed before, so why should this be any different?* Calling yourself a failure and then believing your name-calling does not mean the label you've given yourself is accurate. Check out the facts with yourself and with others.

4. Am I Close Enough to the Situation to Really Know What Is Happening? You may have the thought, *The management of my company does not like my work, and they are probably planning on getting rid of me in the next three months.* How do you know what management is thinking? Are you on the management level? Is your assumption correct? Is your source of information accurate? How can you determine the facts?

5. Am I Thinking in All-or-None Terms? Many people see life as black or white: The world is either great or lousy; people are either all good or all bad; all people are to be feared. Again, where did you get these ideas? What are the facts?

6. Am I Using Ultimatum Words in My Thinking? I must always *be on time, or no one will like me*. That is an unfair statement to make about yourself or anyone else. Notice the following example of how our words can create problems. It is the inner conversation of a woman whose boyfriend left her for another woman. She was attending college where there were numerous other men available.

Negative Thoughts	Answers
He shouldn't have left me for someone else.	I don't like it, but he should have left because he did. For all the reasons I don't know of, he should have left. I don't have to like it, just accept it.
I need him.	I want him back, but I don't need him. I need food, water, and shelter to survive. I don't need a man to survive. Thinking in "needs" makes me vulnerable.
This always happens to me, and it will never change.	Just because it happened in one case doesn't mean it has happened or will happen in every case.
This is terrible, awful, horrible.	These are labels I add to the facts. The labels don't change anything and they make me feel worse.
I must have someone to love me.	It's nice to love and be loved, but making it a condition to being happy is a way of putting myself down.
I'm too ugly and too fat to find anyone else.	"Too" is a relative concept, not some absolute standard. Thinking like this is self-defeating and stops me from trying.
I can't stand being alone.	I can stand difficulties—as I have in the past. I just don't like them.

Negative Thoughts	Answers
I made a fool out of myself.	There's no such thing as a fool. Foolishness is only an abstraction, not something that exists. This mislabeling doesn't do me any good and makes me feel bad.
He made me depressed.	No one can make me feel depressed. I make myself depressed by the way I'm thinking.[2]

7. Am I Taking Examples Out of Context?   A woman overheard the conversation of an instructor talking to another instructor about her. She thought the instructor said she was rigid, pushy, and dominant. Fortunately, she checked out the conversation with one of the two instructors and discovered that she had been described as having high standards and determination. The words were spoken in a positive context, but because of her tendency to think the worst, distortion occurred.

8. Am I Being Honest With Myself?   Am I trying to fool myself or make excuses or put the blame on others?

9. What Is the Source of My Information?   Are your sources accurate, reliable, trustworthy, and do you hear them correctly? Do you ask them to repeat what they say and verify it?

10. What is the Probability of My Thought Occurring?   Perhaps your situation is so rare an occurrence that there is little chance of your worry coming true. One man thought that because he had missed work for two days he would be fired. After he thought about it, he said, "Well, I've worked there for several years and have a good record. When was the last time anyone was fired for missing two days' work? When was the last time they fired anyone?"

11. Am I Assuming Every Situation Is the Same?   Just because you didn't get along at the last two jobs does not mean that you will not get along at your new one. Just because you failed algebra the first time around does not mean you will fail it the second time.

12. Am I Focusing on Irrelevant Factors? Of course there are problems in the world, and people are physically and mentally sick, and crime does exist. What can you do to eliminate these and other problems by sitting around worrying about them or becoming depressed over them? How else could you use your thinking time in a more productive manner?

13. Am I Overlooking My Strengths? People who worry or who are depressed definitely overlook their positive qualities. They do not treat themselves as friends. They are hard on themselves and focus upon their supposed defects instead of identifying their strengths and praising God for them. It is important not only to list your strengths but also to recall times in your past when you were successful.

14. What Do I Want? This is a question I ask people over and over again in counseling. What goals have you set for your life? For your worry? What do you want out of life? How do you want your life to be different? What is the fear that you want to be free from at this point in your life?

15. How Would I Approach This Situation if I Were Not Worrying About it? Would I tend to make it worse than it is? Would I be as immobilized by the problem as I am now? Imagine how you would respond if you believed that you had the capabilities to handle it.

16. What Can I Do to Solve the Situation? Are my thoughts leading to a solution of this problem or making it worse? Have I written down a solution to the problem? When was the last time I tried a different approach?

17. Am I Asking Myself Questions That Have No Answers? Questions like *How can I undo the past? Why did that have to happen? Why can't people be more sensitive?* or, *Why did this happen to me.* Often we can answer questions like these with another question: "Why not?" What if something terrible happens? "So what if it does?" Why spend time asking yourself unanswerable questions?

18. What Are the Distortions in My Own Thinking? The first step in overcoming errors is to identify them. Do you make assumptions or jump to conclusions? What are they?

The best way to deal with an assumption is to check it out. Look for the facts.

19. What Are the Advantages and Disadvantages of Thinking This Way? What are the advantages of worrying? List them on a piece of paper. What are the advantages of thinking that people don't like you? What is the benefit of *any* type of negative thinking?

20. What Difference Will This Make in a Week, a Year, or Ten Years? Will you remember what happened in the future? Five years from now who will remember that your shirt was buttoned wrong? Who really cares? We believe that our mistakes are more important to other people than they really are. If people choose to remember ten years from now, something you said or did that bothered them, that's their problem, not yours.

Your inner dialogue—is it a friend or a foe? Does it control your life, or are you in charge? In this chapter I've passed on a number of suggestions to you, but the most helpful step is still to come. Read on!

Remember:

Identify, analyze, and *reassemble* your thoughts.

If you face a situation involving anger, prepare mentally, think about your inner dialogue beforehand, and take your reaction into account.

When you face rejection, *analyze, reframe* and *rehearse* what you want to say.

Negative thinking need not keep you from giving and receiving praise. Face dysfunctional thoughts with facts.

Energy Builders

1. Are you already in the habit of identifying, analyzing, and reassembling your thoughts? If not, try practicing this when you become aware of negative thoughts.

2. When you face a situation in which you expect anger, do you use the steps outlined here? What were those steps? How

can they help you? Do you have some phrases ready for use in such a situation?

3. When have you faced rejection? Have you used the steps outlined in this chapter? How can you use them in the future?

4. Are you good at giving or receiving praise? Why or why not? How can you change your inner thinking to help you do both better? Use the "Inner-Dialogue Evaluation" to identify your inaccurate thinking.

5. What will you do this week with the information in this chapter? Describe how your communication will be different.

Thirteen

The Most Important Conversation of All— With God

You can't do it by yourself—change your inner dialogue, I mean. Oh, you can try, and you will make *some* progress. But to make major and lasting changes, you must take one final step—converse with God. We call it prayer. We pray because it is our privilege and a means of communication with God the Father. We pray because the Word of God instructs us to pray. As we pray, it's exciting to realize that we are actually welcomed into God's presence: "Let us therefore draw near with confidence to the throne of grace, that we may receive mercy and find grace to help in time of need" (Hebrews 4:16).

Conversation Levels

Since I have a visual bent, I would like to diagram the process which I am suggesting. As you can see from the illustrations.

We Converse With Others

We Converse With Ourselves

We Converse With God

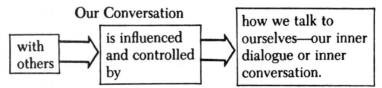

Our Conversation

| with others | → | is influenced and controlled by | → | how we talk to ourselves—our inner dialogue or inner conversation. |

How then do we change our conversations with others?
1. Change our inner dialogue.

HOW?

2. Through our conversation with God.

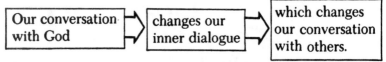

| Our conversation with God | → | changes our inner dialogue | → | which changes our conversation with others. |

Our access to God was made available by Him through His Son Jesus Christ, who died on the cross for us. This was an act of communication on the part of God to the entire world.

We have available to us unbelievable resources for change and growth and stability. But we need to avail ourselves of these resources by conversing with God and allowing Him to talk to us directly and through His Word.

Refashioning Your Thoughts Through Prayer

When you pray, how do you do it? Is it a natural experience for you? Do you use your own language and style of talking, or do you feel you must talk in a certain manner or phrasing in order to get through?

What we pray about is personal, but I would like to recommend one specific prayer: ask God to refashion your thinking. This begins by consecrating your imagination and thought life to God and asking Him to cleanse your thought life of anything that would hinder your growth and progress in life. This suggestion is in keeping with a passage of Scripture found in 1 Peter 1:13 (KJV), "Gird up ... your mind." *Gird* means mental exertion. We are called upon to put out of our minds anything that would hinder the growth and development of our Christian lives. But this growth is accomplished by the working of God in our minds. As believers the Holy Spirit can give us greater awareness of the thoughts that control our lives and greater access to the specific thoughts that need to be changed.

With God's assistance, we can develop a much greater sensitivity to our inner dialogues. On occasion we may feel hesitant to do this, since we feel guilty over an old pattern of thinking. Here again our negative inner dialogues have kept us from honest expression—with God. We need not fear. He will not be surprised or amazed or shocked by anything we say to Him, since He is already aware of our thoughts anyway.

As I have asked people in counseling to commit their inner dialogues to God each day, I have also asked, "How do you envision God responding to admission of your thoughts and pattern of thinking?" This usually provokes not only an interesting response but an indication of the person's image of God.

Admit Your Need

How do we pray then? First we must come to God and admit that our thought lives need renewal and changing. Next, if we lack that desire, we envision Jesus Christ as willing to help us develop the desire to change our thoughts. Often people find it helpful to start the day by asking God to help them identify and dissect their thoughts and then to reassemble them. Although we may or may not be alert to our inner dialogues, we *can* become aware of these conversations. We need to develop the ability to accurately observe them. The Scripture tells us to "bring into captivity every thought to the obedience of Christ" (*see* 2 Corinthians 10:5).

I remember a counselee once who asked me, "Norm, is it all right if I use my imagination in my prayers?" He went on to say, "I find that if I at times actually imagine myself in the presence of Christ, talking to Him, it has a greater impact on my life." I told him it was fine to do so.

Some people derive more benefit out of praying with their eyes open, others by being in a room by themselves and talking out loud. Some individuals who, once they have identified their negative inner dialogue pattern, take each distorted or negative thought, repeat it, and give it over to God. Still others almost act out their prayer by seeing themselves holding each thought in their hands and literally giving it over to Jesus Christ, who accepts it with His hands and takes it away. They conclude this process of prayer by dedicating their imaginations to God in a realistic manner. Actually they have relinquished ownership of their thought lives and imaginations to God. However you do it, whatever method works for you, give your thought life into God's control.

Some people resist this approach because it is so effective! I have found it so in my own life. Some people resist giving God control because they feel comfortable with their negative pattern of thinking, and they know that any effort to change would take time, energy, and patience. In fact, some gain satisfaction from their thinking pattern, which does not follow the direction God desires! Here is a sincere and balanced prayer I once heard:

> Lord, I am at the place of asking You to take over my thought life, my inner dialogues, and my imagination and not only clean them up but give me the power to control my thoughts. I am learning which thoughts cause me the most grief and which ones help me. I have to admit to You that I am a creature of habit, and I know I have spent years developing this type of negative thinking. I do want to communicate better with others and with myself, and I need Your help. I ask You to cause me to be very aware of what I am thinking and its effect. Please remind me, and I will respond to Your prodding. If I revert back to my old way of thinking from time to time, help me not to fall back into being negative about myself because of this lapse. Help me to be patient with myself and with You. Thank You for hearing me, accepting me, and thank You for what You will do for my thought life and inner dialogues in the future.

This man was praying for self-observation, which is one of the important steps involved in changing our inner dialogues. The psalmist said: "Search me, O God, and know my heart; Try me and know my anxious thoughts; And see if there be any hurtful way in me, And lead me in the everlasting way" (Psalms 139:23, 24).

Try Prayer Therapy

Some people find it helpful to conduct their own prayer-therapy sessions for the changing of their thoughts. This involves several uninterrupted hours. Begin the prayer by affirming that the Lord is present, that you are loved by Him, and that you belong to Him. Take a pen and paper. Ask the Lord to guide your mind to inner dialogue statements you make regularly that hinder your relationships with others and with yourself. This is a private time between you and the Lord, and you do not need to rush. If no thoughts come for a while, be patient. As thoughts enter your mind, write them down, but do not evaluate them. After a time, go back over the list and thank Him for allowing you to remember these. Ask God for His wisdom and guidance in changing your thoughts and in becoming aware of them at all times.

I have encouraged a number of individuals to keep a daily log of their thoughts. A log or journal simply records personal insights concerning your thoughts, what you have learned about them, how you have prayed for your thoughts. It also indicates progress in identifying, dissecting, and reconstructing your thoughts. When you write such a journal, you respond to questions such as, "What were the significant thoughts and feelings of this day?" "How did I respond to them?" and you write down the answers. The act of writing something down tells you that it is important.

Another variation of using a log or journal is expressing yourself in prayer. By writing out a prayer or putting it in the form of a letter to God, you give it greater thought and deliberation, and the experience can take on tremendous meaning. You may want to commit yourself to this approach for one week and at the end of that time evaluate what took place.

Some people who face difficult situations in which they usually become very upset spend a few moments prior to the event praying and discussing it with God. During this time they ask God what thoughts He would want them to have. Then they practice those positive thoughts or inner dialogue statements and mentally rehearse them. This is in keeping with Proverbs 15:28, "The heart of the righteous ponders how to answer . . . ," and Proverbs 16:23, "The heart of the wise teaches his mouth. . . ."

The Word of God has so much to say to us about how we should communicate with others. But have you ever considered that some of these same passages need to be applied directly to us first, before we consider them for others?

Conform to God's Image

Scripture says that we are to ". . . encourage . . . one another and edify—strengthen and build up—one another . . ." (1 Thessalonians 5:11 AMP), and we apply this to our response to other individuals. But in order to properly respond to others in this manner, don't we need to respond to ourselves in the same way? In our own thought life do we encourage ourselves, edify and build up ourselves? Or do our thoughts weaken us, disparage and discourage us, and set us up for ineffective communication?

Why do we have such difficulty with our inner dialogue? Many reasons exist, but the most basic is a result of the fall of man and original sin. I believe that one of the outcomes of the fall is an inclination toward negative or distorted thinking, which we will have to confront throughout our lives. Our thoughts are largely responsible for what happens to us. In Proverbs 15:15 (AMP) we read, "All the days of the desponding afflicted are made evil [by anxious thoughts and forboding]. . . ."

But God's purpose is for all of us to conform to the image of His Son. Colossians 3:10 states we are, ". . . being renewed to a true knowledge according to the image of the One who created him." This renewal is a continuing process through sanctification. Sanctification allows us to become what we were created to be, and it is related to our inner dialogue. As we are renewed, our inner dialogues become more Christ-like and less and less like the "old man."

Did you know that your thoughts play a vital role in the sanctification process? Many individuals have compartmentalized their lives. Though they give the outward appearance of having stability and purity, their inward thoughts are a jumbled mess. This inner turmoil has such tight walls around it that it never seeps out, or at least it doesn't when other people are around. Many, many people today live separate inward and outward lives. God's desire for each of us is to be a whole person and no longer fragmented. A double life of the type just described often leads to an explosion or crisis. Why? Because in time the inner thought life gains so much momentum and power that it begins to invade the outer life and soon has overrun that outward life-style and standards. Our thoughts have that much power! Loren Fischer, in *Highway to Dynamic Living*, graphically describes it this way:

> The steam of behavior is only visible proof that the fire of thought is boiling the water of emotion. A heavy lid may curb the steam of action but unless we curb the steam of thinking the heaviest lid possible will blow and high will be the blast of it. Obviously, therefore, we lose spiritual battles not by failing to restrain our actions with the heavier lids, we are defeated because we do not change our flaming thoughts that boil the waters of emotion.

From the pen of Paul, we see this in Ephesians 4:22-25:

> ... that, in reference to your former manner of life, you lay aside the old self, which is being corrupted in accordance with the lusts of deceit, and that you be renewed in the spirit of your mind, and put on the new self, which in the likeness of God has been created in

> righteousness and holiness of the truth. Therefore, laying aside falsehood, speak truth, each one of you, with his neighbor, for we are members of one another.

The renewal he describes here is the spirit of the mind. Under the controlling power of the Holy Spirit, a believer directs his thoughts and energies toward God. "And do not be conformed to this world, but be transformed by the renewing of your mind, that you may prove what the will of God is, that which is good and acceptable and perfect" (Romans 12:2). The renewing of the mind is the adjustment of the person's outlook on life and his thinking process to the mind of God.

In counseling we try to direct a person to focus his thoughts on Christ-like thoughts. "If then you have been raised up with Christ, keep seeking the things above, where Christ is, seated at the right hand of God. Set your mind on the things above, not on the things that are on earth" (Colossians 3:1, 2). "Set your mind on" means to think or focus on. Ephesians 1:18 describes this new outlook as "having the eyes of your heart flooded with light" (AMP).

This is the way to pray then. Ask God to flood the eyes of your heart with light, since the heart is the core or center of your inmost self; your feelings, words, and actions stem from your heart. Enlightened eyes come through the work and power of the Holy Spirit. The power a believer has available to him or her is the same power God used to raise Christ from the dead! As this power translates to your mind or thought life, realize that God gives us the ability to picture things the way He pictures them. We all need a transformation of the mind to have the mind of Christ.

In a recent sermon, Lloyd Ogilvie, pastor of the First Presbyterian Church of Hollywood, said, "Each of us needs to surrender the kingdom of our mind to God." Have you done that? Have you surrendered your mind to be a resting place for the Spirit of God? When you do, your inner dialogue can change, and your outer conversations will reflect the difference. Your listening and talking and your ability to speak another person's language and become an encourager will take on a new dimension.

So you see, becoming a total listener does not just rely on you and your communication with others! Instead, it is based on you and the person of Jesus Christ! Jesus Christ is the creator of positive effective communication!

Remember:

We converse on three levels: with others, with ourselves, and with God.

God can refashion your thoughts if you commit yourself to prayer and a renewal of your thought life that will conform you to the image of His Son.

Energy Builders

1. What are the three levels of dialogue? How does each affect your ability to be a total listener?

2. How can prayer change your inner dialogue? What step do you have to take? If you need to, take that step.

3. Spend some time in prayer therapy or in writing a journal of prayer. What have you discovered about yourself? About your communication with God? With others? Are you open to God's sanctification?

4. What will you do this week with the information in this chapter. Describe how your communication will be different.

Source Notes ─────────────

Chapter 2

1. David Augsburger, *Caring Enough to Hear* (Ventura, Calif.: Regal Books, 1982), 41, 42.

Chapter 4

1. Matthew McKay, Martha Davis, and Patrick Fanning, *Messages* (Oakland, Calif.: New Harbinger Pubs. 1983), 42.
2. Ibid., 70–78.

Chapter 7

1. Robert Bolton and Dorothy Grover Bolton, *Social Style/Management Style—Developing Productive Work*

Relationships (New York: American Management Association, 1984), 11, 12.

2. For additional information, contact Center for Social Style Research and Application, Rudge Consultants, 5 Ledhard Avenue, Cazenovia, New York 13035, (315) 655-3393.

3. Jerry Richardson and Joel Margulis, *The Magic of Rapport* (San Francisco: Harbor Pub., 1981) 19-30, 51-56, adapted.

Chapter 8

1. Robert Dilts, *Applications of Neuro-Linguistic Programming* (Cupertino, Calif.: Meta Pubs. 1983), Chapter 1, 3-15; Chapter 2, 5, adapted.

2. Charles Swindoll, *Growing Strong in the Seasons of Life* (Portland, Ore.: Multnomah Press, 1983), 132.

3. Ibid., 61.

4. Mike Samuels and Nancy Samuels, *Seeing With the Mind's Eye* (New York: Random House, 1975), 169.

5. Dilts, *Neuro-Linguistic Programming*, 9, 10, adapted.

Chapter 9

1. Ed and Carol Neuenschwander, *Two Friends in Love* (Portland, Ore.: Multnomah Press, 1986), 135.

2. Ken Druck with James C. Simmons, *The Secrets Men Keep* (New York: Doubleday & Co., 1985), 35, 36, adapted.

3. Ibid., 39, 40, adapted.

Chapter 10

1. Don Dinkmeyer and Lewis Losoncy, *The Encouragement Book* (Englewood Cliffs, N. J.: Prentice-Hall Inc., 1980), 70-78, adapted.

2. Don Dinkmeyer and Gary McKay, *Raising a Responsible Child* (New York: Simon & Schuster, 1973), 99-101.

Chapter 11

1. Lloyd John Ogilvie, *Why Not? Accept Christ's Healing and Wholeness* (Old Tappan, N. J.: Fleming H. Revell, 1985) 66

2. Matthew McKay, Martha Davis, Patrick Fleming, *Thoughts and Feelings* (Richmond, Calif., New Harbinger Pubs., 1981), 26, adapted.

Chapter 12

1. Raymond W. Novaco, *Anger Control* (Lexington, Mass.: Lexington Books, D.C. Heath & Co., 1975), as used in Patricia Jakubowski and Arthur J. Lange. *The Assertive Option* (Champaign, Ill.: Research Press, 1978), 148, 151, adapted.
2. Gary Emery, *A New Beginning: How You Can Change Your Thoughts Through Cognitive Therapy* (New York: Simon & Schuster, 1981), 61.